I0755607

THE

BAPTIST CHURCH DIRECTORY.

A GUIDE TO THE

DOCTRINES AND DISCIPLINE,

OFFICERS AND ORDINANCES,

PRINCIPLES AND PRACTICES,

OF

BAPTIST CHURCHES.

EMBRACING A CONCISE VIEW OF THE QUESTIONS OF

BAPTISM AND COMMUNION.

BY

EDWARD T. HISCOX, D.D.,

PASTOR OF STANTON STREET BAPTIST CHURCH, NEW YORK.

SEVENTH THOUSAND.

NEW YORK:

SHELDON & COMPANY.

BOSTON: GOULD & LINCOLN.

1859.

PREFACE.

The following is designed, as its name implies, to be a directory to the doctrines and practices of Baptist churches. Its plan is different from that of any other work; more comprehensive in the range of its subjects, but more concise in its statement of facts. It is rather a book for reference than a book for general reading. The arrangement is intended to be so clear and convenient, that any subject on which information is wanted, can be found at once. The style is adapted to the condition of those who desire information on such subjects, but who have little disposition for laborious or protracted investigation—instances of which are frequently occurring within the observation of every pastor.

There are great numbers of the younger members of our churches who, while they have a deep conviction that the doctrines they hold are according to the word of God, yet greatly need instruction as to church order and discipline, and the usages of the denomination. Indeed, there are many older members who might not be able to bring forward arguments to justify their faith and practice, or give information to those who desire to be instructed as to our denominational peculiarities. Besides, there are many outside the churches who often wish to know accurately what Baptists do believe and practise. These persons have, perhaps, small means to purchase, and little time to peruse many books. They desire to have the whole matter so condensed and definite that they can see it at a glance, and so reliable that they cannot doubt its correctness. The Directory is designed to supply this want.

Proof sheets of it were sent by the publishers to a number of ministers, eminent for learning and piety, residing in different sections of the country, who were requested to express their opinions of its merits, and also to make any suggestions that might improve it. I take this opportunity to express my gratitude for the very kind and generous terms in which they were pleased to speak of it, as well as for the very valuable suggestions, which were made by several of them —which suggestions have, to a considerable degree, been adopted.

It is hoped that this work, prepared with much labor and care, and having met such general and generous approval, will be thought worthy to find a place in every church, and to be in the hands of every church member. That it may, by the divine blessing, contribute to the harmony, peace, and prosperity of our churches, is my sincere desire and prayer.

E. T. H.

NEW YORK, *February* 22, 1859.

CONTENTS.

PART FIRST.

CHAPTER I.

A CHURCH.

CHAPTER II.

ITS OFFICERS.

CHAPTER III.

ITS ORDINANCES.

CHAPTER IV.

ITS SERVICES.

CHAPTER V.

ITS WORSHIP.

CHAPTER VI.

ITS GOVERNMENT.

CHAPTER VII.

ITS MINISTRY.

CHAPTER VIII.

ITS MEMBERSHIP.

CHAPTER IX.

ITS DISCIPLINE.

CHAPTER X.

ITS BUSINESS.

CHAPTER XI.

ITS MISSION.

CHAPTER XII.

ITS CUSTOMS.

CHAPTER XIII.

ITS DUTIES.

CHAPTER XIV.

ITS PRIVILEGES.

CHAPTER XV.

ITS PIETY.

CHAPTER XVI.

ITS DOCTRINES.

PART SECOND.

CHAPTER I.

DENOMINATIONAL PECULIARITIES. PAGE

CHAPTER II.

THE BAPTISMAL QUESTION.

CHAPTER III.

THE QUESTION OF INFANT BAPTISM.

CHAPTER IV.

. THE COMMUNION QUESTION.

CHAPTER V.

QUESTION OF CHURCH OFFICERS.

CHAPTER VI.

QUESTION OF CHURCH GOVERNMENT.

CHAPTER VII.

BAPTIST HISTORY.

CHAPTER VIII.

FORMS AND BLANKS.

CHAPTER IX.

BENEVOLENT SOCIETIES.

THE

BAPTIST CHURCH DIRECTORY.

PART FIRST.

CHAPTER I.

A CHURCH.

I.—WHAT IS A CHRISTIAN CHURCH?

A Christian Church is *a congregation of baptized believers in Christ*, worshipping together; associated in the faith and fellowship of the Gospel; practising its precepts; observing its ordinances; recognizing and receiving Christ as their supreme lawgiver and ruler; and taking his Word as their sufficient and exclusive rule of faith and practice, in all matters of religion.

That a Christian Church is a congregation of Christian disciples, and not a society, or number of congregations or churches combined, and united under some more general head or government, is evident from the Scriptural mention made of the Apostolic churches. There were "the churches throughout all Judea, and Galilee, and Samaria;"[1] also "the church which was in Jerusalem;"[2] they "ordained them elders in every church;"[3] "the churches of Galatia;"[4] "the churches of Asia;"[5] "the churches of Macedonia;"[6] "the church of the Laodiceans;"[7] "the church of the Thessalonians;"[8] "the church that is at Babylon."[9]

Though *the church* is sometimes spoken of, in distinction from the world, as the church universal, embracing all the people of God everywhere, yet by *churches* are meant single, separate, visible congregations of Christian disciples, definitely organized, with their laws, officers, ordinances, discipline, and duties, doing the work and maintaining the worship of Christ. A church is "the body" in its relation to Christ who is "the head." It is "a spiritual temple," as being composed of spiritual or regenerate members, and distinguished from all material and unsanctified organizations. It is "the pillar and ground of the truth," in its relation to the maintenance and support of the divine law, and

[1] Acts ix. 31. [2] Acts xi. 22. [3] Acts xiv. 23.
[4] 1 Cor. xvi. 1. [5] 1 Cor. xvi. 19. [6] 2 Cor. viii. 1.
[7] Col. iv. 16. [8] 1 Thes. i. 1. [9] 1 Peter v. 13.

its proclamation and propagation of the great realities of the Gospel.

1. *The Character of Churches.*—A church constitutes a kind of spiritual kingdom in the world, but not of the world; whose king is Christ; whose law is his word; whose institutions are his ordinances; whose duty is his service; whose reward is his blessing.

In all matters of faith and conscience, as well as in all matters of internal order and government, a church is "under law to Christ;"[1] but as men and citizens, its members must "submit themselves to governors,"[2] like other men, so far as shall not interfere with, or contravene, the claims of the divine law and authority upon them.[3]—They must "render unto Cesar the things that are Cesar's, and unto God the things that are God's,"[4] remembering that God's claims are supreme, and annihilate all claims that contradict or oppose them.

2. *The Design of Churches.*—The evident design of our Saviour in founding and preserving churches in the world, was, that they should be monuments in the midst of guilty men, bearing perpetual witness against the wickedness of the world, and to the goodness of God. But espe-

[1] 1 Cor. ix. 21.
[2] 1 Peter ii. 14.
[3] See Part First, chap. vi.
[4] Matt. xxii. 21.

cially that they should be living testimonies to the work of redemption, "the light of the world," and "the salt of the earth."[1]

They constitute the effective instrumentality by which the will of God and the knowledge of salvation through Christ are made known to men; at the same time they form homes for the saints on earth; sheep-folds for the safety of the flock, and schools for the instruction and training of the children of the covenant; while they encourage the penitent and warn the careless. Churches should well understand their "high calling," and seek to accomplish it, "according to the will of God."[2]

3. *The Authority of Churches.*—The authority of a church is limited to its own members, and applies to all matters of Christian character, and whatever involves the welfare of religion. It is designed to secure in all its members a conduct and conversation "becoming godliness."

This authority is derived directly from God; not from states, nor princes, nor people; not from its own officers, nor its members, nor from any other source of ecclesiastical or civil power or right.[3] But Christ "is head over all things to the church,"[4] and also as of right, "the church

[1] Matt. v. 13, 14.
[2] Gal. i. 4.
[3] See Part First, chap. vi.—Second Part, chap. vi.
[4] Eph. i. 22.

is subject to Christ."[1] But the authority of the church does not extend to its own members even, in matters merely personal and temporal, and which do not affect their character or duties as Christians.[2]

II.—Churches Constituted.

When a number of Christians, members of the same or of different churches, believe that their own spiritual improvement, or the religious welfare of the community so requires, they organize a new church.

This is done by uniting in mutual covenant, to sustain the relations and obligations prescribed by the Gospel, to be governed by the laws of Christ's house, and to maintain public worship and the preaching of the Gospel. Articles of faith are usually adopted, as also a name by which the church shall be known, and its officers elected.

III.—Churches Recognized.

It is customary for them to call a council, to meet at the same, or at a subsequent time, to *recognize* them; that is, to examine their doctrines, inquire into the circumstances and reasons of their organization, and express, on behalf

[1] Eph. v. 24. [2] See Part First, chaps. viii., ix.

of the churches they represent, approbation for their course, and fellowship for them, as a regularly constituted church of the same denomination. The calling of a council is, however, entirely optional with the church; it is a prudential measure merely, to secure the sympathy and approbation of sister churches, but is in no sense necessary.

The council usually hear their articles of faith and covenant; listen to a statement of the causes which led to their organization; examine the letters held by the constituent members; carefully consider the whole subject, and then vote their approval, if they so approve, or advise them to the contrary, if they disapprove. It is customary to hold some appropriate religious service on the occasion, when a *discourse* is preached, a *charge* given to the church, the *hand of fellowship* extended by the council to the church, through some one chosen by each for the service.

NOTE 1.—A church may fail in some respects to meet the requirements of the Gospel, and still be a Church of Christ, providing it fulfills the fundamental conditions of a scriptural faith and practice.

NOTE 2.—But when a church ceases to acknowledge and submit to Christ as its supreme ruler, and to receive his Word as its supreme law, then it ceases to be a Church of Christ, though it may still accept some of his doctrines and practise some of his precepts.

NOTE 3.—If a council should refuse to recognize a newly constituted church, still that church would have the right to maintain their organization, and continue the forms of worship, and would as really be a church without, as with the sanction of the council. It would seldom, however, be expedient to do this, against the convictions of churches and pastors expressed in the decisions of a council.

NOTE 4.—The multiplication of feeble churches should be guarded against, and the organization of new interests without the prospect of becoming independent and efficient, should be discouraged.

NOTE 5.—Especially ought the formation of new churches, as the outgrowth and fruit of strife and dissension in older ones, to be avoided and discountenanced, except in the most extreme cases. A large and careful observation proves, that very few churches so constituted ever attain to any considerable degree of prosperity, or usefulness.

NOTE 6.—It not unfrequently happens, that a council doubts the propriety of recognizing a new church, and yet hesitates to refuse lest it might possibly place difficulties in their way, and hinder the progress of a good cause. In such cases the more wise and prudent course is, for the council to adjourn for a specified time, three or six months, at the end of which the case would be likely to present a more definite aspect, and allow of a more satisfactory decision.

CHAPTER II.

ITS OFFICERS.

The scriptural *officers* of a church are *two:* Pastor, and Deacon.

I.—The Pastor.

In the New Testament the pastor is called *bishop*, which means an *overseer*, and indicates the nature of his work. He is also called *elder*, or *presbyter*, which properly means an aged person—a term probably derived from the Jewish synagogue, and indicates dignity of office. He is also called a *minister*, which means a *servant*, and implies that he is to *minister* and serve in spiritual things. The term *pastor* signifies a *shepherd*, and implies also the nature of the relations he sustains to the church.

1. *His Duties.*—The pastor is to take the oversight of the church in spiritual things. His special duties are, preaching the Gospel, administering the ordinances, carefully watching over,

[1] See First Part, chap. vii., Second Part, chap. v.

guiding, and advancing the religious interests of the people, "for the perfecting of the saints, for the work of the ministry, for the edifying of the body of Christ."[1]

2. *His Authority.*—Though pastors cannot rightfully assume authority as being "lords over God's heritage,"[2] yet there is a sense in which the ministerial office should command and receive a deference rendered to no other. The Apostle enjoins that "the elders that rule well be counted worthy of double honor,"[3] and, also, to "obey them that have the rule over you, and submit yourselves."[4] Here is a sense, therefore, in which they are to *rule*, and the people are to *obey*.

3. *His Sphere.*—A minister should do good everywhere, "as he has opportunity." But his special and particular sphere of labor is with "the flock over which the Holy Ghost hath made them overseers, to feed the church of God;"[5] "taking the oversight thereof not by constraint, but willingly, not for filthy lucre, but of a ready mind."[6] Nothing else should be allowed to interfere with the completeness and fidelity of his duties to the people of his charge.

[1] Eph. iv. 12. [2] 1 Peter v. 3. [3] 1 Tim. v. 17.
[4] Heb. xiii. 17. [5] Acts xx. 18. [6] 1 Peter v. 2.

NOTE 1.—In choosing a pastor, the utmost care is requisite. Great prudence and discretion are needed, especially on the part of deacons and leading members of the church. An act so vitally connected with the welfare of the church and the prosperity of the Gospel, should be preceded and accompanied by earnest and protracted prayer for divine direction in the choice.

NOTE 2.—One should be selected who gives undoubted evidence of having been called of God to the holy work: one on whom the church can unite, and with whom they can coöperate, and who also possesses qualifications fitted for that particular field. A man of deep and undoubted piety, the integrity and consistency of whose conduct command the confidence of all who know him, and whose usefulness is hindered by no moral or social defect.

NOTE 3.—The connection between pastor and church is sometimes made for a limited and specified time; but more commonly it is indefinite, and can be terminated at the request of either party. *Permanency* in the pastoral relation should most earnestly be sought, as tending to the welfare of all concerned. Trifling disadvantages should rather be endured than remedied at the expense of those more serious evils, which frequent changes seldom fail to bring upon both church and pastor.

NOTE 4.—In settling a pastor, the church either calls a young man to be ordained, or one who is already in the ministry. In the *first case*, they should be well acquainted with the character of the candidate, and be satisfied with his reputation for piety, and also have sufficient opportunities of hearing him preach, to judge whether his gifts promise usefulness in that field. In the *second case*, they should be informed as to the history of his past labors, and know that he has a good report of the people of his charge, and especially of those who are without. A minister who does not command the respect of society, cannot be very useful in the church.

NOTE 5.—Is it right and proper for one church to call a man to be their pastor who is at the time pastor of another church? Merely to call a man would neither be wrong nor dishonorable —would violate no law of christian right or courtesy. Let the responsibility then rest with *him* of deciding whether it is right and expedient to accept the call. But if one church should use special means to unsettle the pastor of another, by arguments, persuasions, and inducements, it would be both unchristian and dishonorable.

NOTE 6.—The too common practice of hearing many *candidates* preach *on trial* cannot be approved, and usually operates most unfavorably upon the church which practises it. A few sermons, preached under such circumstances, are no just indication of a man's ministerial ability, or pastoral qualifications. It shows little more than the manner of his address. His general reputation, and the history of his past successes, will afford a more correct estimate of his worth and adaptation.

II.—THE DEACONS.

The term *deacon* in the New Testament means properly, a *minister*, or *servant*, and is applied to the Apostles, and even to Christ himself. But in ecclesiastical usage it designates an officer in the church.

1. *Their Origin.*—The account of the institution of this office is found in Acts vi. 1–6. When the number of converts was greatly multiplied, the care of the needy, and the charge of temporal affairs added so much to the labors of the Apostles as seriously to interfere with their spiritual duties. Hence having called the

multitude of the disciples together, they stated the case, and requested them to select "*seven men of honest report, full of the Holy Ghost, and wisdom,*" to perform this work, that they might "give themselves continually to prayer, and to the ministry of the word." These were accordingly selected, when the Apostles set them apart to the service for which they were chosen, by the laying on of hands, with prayer.

2. *Their Duties.*—The deacons, therefore, are to be chosen from among the faithful, prudent, and experienced members by a free vote of the church. Their duties are, the care of the sick and needy members, having charge of the temporal affairs of the church, counselling with, and assisting the pastor in advancing the welfare of the body.

3. *Their Number.*—Their number is variable and discretionary; usually from *two* to *seven*, according to the condition and necessities of the church, the latter being the original scriptural number. The number, however, should not be increased merely as a form, nor out of compliment to the men, but for the sake of actual and substantial service to be performed by them.

4. *Their Period.*—They are sometimes chosen for a *limited*, but more commonly for an *indefi-*

nite period, their places to be filled by others whenever they or the church may desire. Permanency in this as well as the pastoral, usually tends to secure a higher regard for the office, and greater usefulness on the part of those who fill it.

5. *Their Ordination.*—In the Apostolic example deacons were *ordained* with the solemn service of laying on of hands. In our older churches, this practice was carefully adhered to, as it still is very generally at the South, but in many parts, of late, it has fallen very much into disuse. The office is coming to be far too lightly esteemed, and the scriptural character of the men is too little insisted on. Ordination, if practised, would invest both with more importance. Too much care cannot be given to secure the right kind of men, when we consider that the permanent influence of a deacon for good or evil in a church, is scarcely surpassed by that of the pastor himself.

NOTE 1.—It will be observed that the *deaconship* was not instituted by Christ, but by the Apostles, and grew out of the emergencies of the case. That it was divinely approved, however, and intended to be permanent, is evident, since Paul subsequently recognizes the office, and specifies the qualifications which deacons shall possess.

NOTE 2.—It will be noticed also, that the deacons were

chosen by the *church*, that is, the "multitude of the disciples," and chosen also from among their own number; but were *ordained*, or appointed, by the Apostles, with prayer and laying on of hands.

NOTE 3.—The *qualifications* made requisite in the men sufficiently indicate the importance of the office, and the care with which it should be filled. "Men of honest report—full of the Holy Ghost, and wisdom." While in 1 Tim. chap. iii., the qualifications required are much the same as those mentioned in the case of bishops or pastors.

NOTE 4.—It is evident from the character of the men, and the personal history of some of them, that while a care for the temporal interests of the church was to constitute the distinctive feature of their office and duties; at the same time they were foremost as counsellors and coadjutors with the Apostles, for the *spiritual* interests of the church. Having been among the most devout, prudent, and faithful, before their election, and as the reason for their being chosen, they would not be less so, afterwards. Such should the deacons ever be.

NOTE 5.—The *deaconesses* referred to in 1 Tim. iii. 11, were, probably, not deacons' wives, but a class of females appointed in the churches, to minister to the sick, and perform other services to those of their own sex, which could more appropriately be done by them than by the male members.

III.—OTHER OFFICERS.

It is usual for a church, as a matter of convenience, to appoint a *Clerk* to take minutes, and preserve records of its business proceedings, with all other records and papers belonging to it. Also, a *Treasurer* is chosen, to hold, disburse, and account for moneys for church purposes. Also, *Trustees* are elected where they may be necessary, legally to hold property, and administer its financial affairs, and when so required by the laws of the State.

But these are the appointments of *expediency*, and are not scriptural church officers. The duties of the officers just mentioned do properly belong to the deacons, and constitute a part of their appropriate work. Yet it may be right, and needful, to distribute the labors and burdens of the church among its members, as also to meet any requirements of civil law.

NOTE 1.—The various duties and responsible services of the church should be as widely distributed among the members as practicable, so that the same persons need not fill different offices at the same time. This will avoid imposing heavy burdens on a few, accustom all to responsible duties, and guard against committing the official influence and control of the body into the hands of a few members.

NOTE 2.—The trustees are really a standing committee of the church appointed for a specific purpose. They are therefore entirely under the direction of the church, and not separate from, nor independent of the body. They cannot hold, use, nor dispose of the property placed in their hands, except as instructed by the church. Whatever technical rights or privileges civil laws or the decisions of courts may give them, they are bound by every principle of honor, morality and religion, strictly to perform the wishes and obey the instructions of the church by which they are appointed.

CHAPTER III.

ITS ORDINANCES.

THE *Ordinances* enjoined by the Gospel, and to be observed by a Christian Church, are *two: Baptism* and the *Lord's Supper*. These are the two symbols of the new covenant, the two pillars of the spiritual temple, the two monuments of the new dispensation. Christ has appointed no others. They are *positive* institutions, as distinguished from those of a simply *moral* character; and their force and sacredness, together with the obligation to honor and observe them, come directly from the character and authority of Christ who appointed them.

I.—BAPTISM.[1]

Baptism is the *immersion* of the candidate in water, in or into the name of the Father, Son, and Holy Spirit; and is administered to *such only*, as profess faith in Christ, giving evidence of a regenerate heart.

[1] See Second Part, chap. ii.

1. *Its Institution.*—Baptism was instituted by Christ, or by John the Baptist admitting his baptism, to be Christian Baptism. It did not come in place of circumcision, or any other sign or seal of the old covenant, but was ordained for the new. Thus "John did baptize in the wilderness and preached the baptism of repentance for the remission of sins."[1] "Then cometh Jesus from Galilee to Jordan unto John, to be baptized of him."[2] "And Jesus, when he was baptized, went up straightway out of the water."[3] "And he said to his disciples, Go ye therefore and teach all nations, baptizing them in the name of the Father, and of the Son, and of the Holy Ghost."[4]

2. *Its Administration.*[5]—The form or manner of its administration, is that of *dipping*, or immersing the person to be baptized, in water, and is thereby distinguished from the many ablutions and sprinklings of the Mosaic dispensation. "And they went down both into the water, both Philip and the Eunuch, and he baptized him."[6] "Therefore we are buried with him by baptism, into death."[7] "Buried with him in baptism."[8]

3. *Its Subjects.*—It is to be administered to

[1] Mark i. 4. [2] Matt. iii. 13. [3] Matt. iii. 16.
[4] Matt. xxviii. 19 [5] See Part Second, chap. ii. [6] Acts viii. 38.
[7] Rom. vi. 4. [8] Col. ii. 12.

such, and only such, as have exercised godly repentance for sin, and a saving faith in Christ. "But when they believed they were baptized both men and women."[1] "Then they that gladly received his word were baptized."[2] "If thou believest with all thy heart, thou mayest."[3]

4. *Its Obligation.*—Every person is under the most solemn obligation to repent and believe in Christ; and every believer in Christ is under solemn obligation to be baptized into his name. No one who trusts in him for salvation can lightly esteem his authority, or willingly disregard his command, or neglect to profess the faith exercised, by submitting to this ordinance. "Repent and be baptized, every one of you, in the name of Jesus Christ."[4] "Arise and be baptized, and wash away thy sins."[5]

5. *It is Commemorative.*—Baptism points perpetually to Christ in his humiliation, death, and resurrection, and keeps constantly in the minds of candidates and observers, him "who died for our sins, and rose again for our justification." It witnesses and testifies that he suffered, died, was buried, and rose from the dead, to perfect the work of redemption. "So many of us as were baptized into Christ were baptized

[1] Acts viii. 12. [2] Acts ii. 41. [3] Acts viii. 36.
[4] Acts ii. 38. [5] Acts xxii. 16.

into his death."[1] "Buried with him in baptism wherein also ye are risen with him."[2] There is "one Lord, one faith, one baptism;"[3] thus forever connecting the Lord with his disciple, by the living links of faith and baptism. "We are buried with him by baptism into death."[4]

6. *It is Typical.*—It points out things to come, and prefigures most beautifully, the resurrection of the body from the dead, "like as Christ was raised up from the dead, by the glory of the Father,"[5] in which doctrine of the resurrection the candidate symbolically professes his faith. "If the dead rise not at all, why are they then baptized for the dead."[6] Thus uniting the hope of the future to the faith of the past, and binding both to the realities of the present, in baptism.

7. *It is Emblematic.*—It is a confession of the great cardinal doctrines of the Gospel. In the symbolic force and expression of the ordinance, the mode of it is emphatic. No other manner could teach these doctrines. It represents Christ's sufferings, death, and burial, for our sins, and his resurrection from the dead for our justification. "But I have a baptism to be baptized with; and how am I straitened till it be accomplished."[7] It represents the candidate's

[1] Rom. vi. 3. [2] Col. ii. 12. [3] Eph. iv. 5. [4] Rom. vi. 4.
[5] Rom. vi. 4. [6] 1 Cor. xv. 29. [7] Luke xii. 50.

death to sin, and rising to a new spiritual life in Christ; "Buried with him by baptism into death."[1] "For as many as have been baptized into Christ, have put on Christ."[2]

It professes hope in the resurrection from the dead: "For if we have been planted together in the likeness of his death, we shall be also in the likeness of his resurrection."[3] The life everlasting stands in sacred fellowship with the death to sin; for, "if we be dead with Christ, we believe that we shall also live with him."[4] It represents in an outward symbol the inward work of the Spirit, and shows how, "according to his mercy, he saved us by the washing of regeneration, and the renewing of the Holy Ghost,"[5] a work already performed upon the heart of the candidate, by an application of the cleansing blood of Christ. "The like figure whereunto even Baptism doth now save us (not the putting away the filth of the flesh, but the answer of a good conscience towards God), by the resurrection of Jesus Christ."[6]

It also shows forth the unity of the faith and the fellowship of the people of God, who in the one baptism, profess their trust in the one Lord, and their acceptance of the one faith: "For

[1] Rom. vi. 4. [2] Gal. iii. 27. [3] Rom. vi. 5.
[4] Rom. vi. 8. [5] Tit. iii. 5. [6] 1 Peter iii. 21.

by one Spirit we are all baptized into one body." [1]

II.—The Lord's Supper.[2]

The Lord's Supper is a provision of bread and wine, as symbols of Christ's body and blood, partaken by the members of the church, to commemorate his sufferings and death, and to show their faith and participation in the merits of his sacrifice.

1. *Its Institution.*—Our Saviour instituted the Supper at the close of the last paschal feast which he kept with the disciples before he suffered. "As they were eating, Jesus took bread and blessed it, and brake it, and gave it to the disciples, and said, Take eat; this is my body. And he took the cup and gave thanks, and gave it to them saying, Drink ye all of it; for this is my blood, of the New Testament, which is shed for many for the remission of sins." [3]

2. *Its Obligation.*—It is not only a privilege for the Christian to receive the Supper, but it is his duty. It is the duty of every believer to be baptized, and the duty of every baptized believer to receive the communion of the Supper. "Take, eat; drink ye all of it." "Divide it among

[1] 1 Cor. xii. 13. [2] See First Part, chap. xiv. 3.—Second Part, chap. iv.
[3] Matt. xxvi. 26.

yourselves." "This do in remembrance of me."[1] Let no disciple lightly esteem it.

3. *Its Subjects.*[2]—Those who have a right to the supper are baptized believers, who are walking according to his Word and will. No others. Our Saviour "sat down, and his twelve Apostles with him,"[3] and he "gave it to the disciples,"[4] not to others, and said, "Take this and divide it among yourselves,"[5] not among others.

4. *It is Commemorative.*—It is designed to commemorate the death of Christ, and be a perpetual memorial in his churches, and to his people, of his sacrifice for their redemption. "This do, in remembrance of me;" "This do ye, as oft as ye drink it, in remembrance of me."[6]

5. *It is Typical.*—It not only points the Christian back to the broken body, and the blood shed, to the Saviour's sufferings and death, but onward, also, to his second coming, and the feast and fellowship above. "But I say unto you, I will not drink henceforth of this fruit of the vine, until that day when I drink it new with you, in my Father's kingdom;"[7] "For as often as ye eat this bread, and drink this cup, ye do show the Lord's death, till he come."[8]

[1] Luke xxii. 16. [2] See Second Part, chap. iv.
[3] Luke xxii. 14. [4] Matt. xxvi. 26. [5] Luke xxii. 17.
[6] 1 Cor. xi. 24, 25. [7] Matt. xxvi. 29. [8] 1 Cor. xi. 26.

6. *It is Emblematic.*—In all these things it teaches symbolically great Gospel truths, while it perpetuates the memory of the work of redemption, by the death of Christ. It is the sign or seal, of the love of Christ to the believer in the new covenant of grace, and a token of his faithfulness. "This cup is the new testament in my blood."[1]

It shows a spiritual fellowship and communion with Christ, on the part of those who receive it, and indicates their union with him; "The cup of blessing which we bless, is it not the communion of the blood of Christ? The bread which we break, is it not the communion of the body of Christ?"[2]

It expresses, also, a fellowship of the disciples for each other, and a unity of faith on the part of those who receive it. They, though many, are one body, and Christ is the one head; "for we, being many, are one bread and one body; for we are all partakers of that one bread."[3]

It represents the spiritual life and nourishment of the Christian, as derived wholly from Christ, through faith in him, as life and nourishment for the body are derived from common bread and wine; "For even Christ our passover, is sacri-

[1] Luke xxii. 20. [2] 1 Cor. x. 16. [3] 1 Cor. x. 17

ficed for us. Therefore let us keep the feast: not with old leaven, but with the unleavened bread of sincerity and truth."[1]

NOTE 1.—In baptizing candidates, the utmost decorum, good order, and solemnity should be observed, and nothing on the part, either of the administrator, or the candidates occur to excite any other emotions in the minds of spectators, than those of reverence and devotion. Sometimes this most impressive and sacred ordinance is administered so rudely, with such thoughtless haste, and with so many blunders and mistakes, as to bring it into great disrespect in the estimation of those who witness it.

NOTE 2.—Both ordinances are usually administered by *ministers;* but should the church so direct, would doubtless be valid if administered by a private member of the church.

NOTE 3.—It is not pretended that there is any spiritual power or efficacy in the ordinances, to purify or sanctify the soul; but as divinely appointed, they certainly are means of grace, the use of which tends greatly to spiritual profit, when performed with faith, and the neglect of which, is a disobedience and a cause of spiritual decline.

NOTE 4.—These ordinances are usually administered on the Sabbath, and more commonly once each month—particularly the Supper. They may however be administered at any time or place at the discretion of the church as circumstances may require.

NOTE 5.—Baptism, properly speaking, is *not to be repeated* But in cases where baptism in form has been administered, evidently without the exercise of a saving faith, and without even an intelligent profession of such a faith on the part of the candidate, and without a correct understanding of the nature and

[1] 1 Cor. v. 7, 8.

requirements of the Gospel, or the design of the ordinance itself, as also where the administrator was not duly qualified—in such cases the ordinance may be repeated. This would be re-baptizing in form, but not in fact, since in the first case the ordinance being invalidated, was not really a Scriptural baptism.

NOTE 6.--It is customary for the pastor, on communion occasions, when the Table is spread, and just before the administration of the ordinance, to invite "all persons in good and regular standing in churches of the same faith and order" to sit down and partake with them. Some, however, give no invitation at all; and some invite only the members of that particular church, holding that none should enjoy the privileges of the communion in any church, except those who are under the watch-care and discipline of that church.

NOTE 7.—Strictly speaking, the privileges of a church are coëxtensive with the authority of the church; and the *right* of communing, therefore, is limited to those over whom the church exercises the right of discipline. Consequently the *right* to commune in any church is confined to the members of that particular church; and if the members of other churches are at any time invited, it is a mere matter of courtesy extended to them.

NOTE 8.—The Supper being a church ordinance, it would not be proper to administer it in a *sick room*, or in other places, privately, without the knowledge or sanction of the church. But the church has a right to authorize and direct its administration in any place, or on any occasion, itself being present as a body, or represented by some of its officers and members.

NOTE 9.—A neglect of the Communion by church members is a very grave evil. It is without excuse, and operates most unfavorably on the piety of those who do it. It casts indignity upon the church and the ordinance of Christ, and is a breach of good order which the church should endeavor promptly to correct. Some churches, by a rule of discipline, visit each member who absents himself twice in succession from the Lord's Supper.

CHAPTER IV.

ITS SERVICES.

The *services* of a church are mostly devotional; the order and arrangement of which are not fixed by any scriptural precept, or precedent, but are to be determined by the church itself.[1]

I.—Preaching the Gospel.

Usually, *two* discourses are preached on the Sabbath; sometimes *three;* sometimes only *one.* In many churches also, a *lecture* is given on some evening during the week.

The *order* of service is usually this: 1, singing; 2, reading the Scriptures; 3, prayer; 4, singing; 5, preaching; 6, prayer; 7, singing; 8, benediction. But the relative order is arranged usually according to the taste of the minister who performs the service.

II.—Social Meetings.

During the week, *once* or *twice*, meetings are

[1] See Part First, chap. vi.

held, where each member, without distinction, is at liberty, though not compelled, to take part in services of prayer, praise, and exhortation.

III.—Covenant Meetings.

In most churches, once each month, a Covenant Meeting is held, at which all the members are desired to speak of their religious experience during the month past, and express their fellowship with the church.

IV.—Church Meetings.

Once a month, also, a Church Meeting is usually held, for the transaction of business; such as receiving, dismissing, or disciplining members, and any other necessary to be done. *Special* church meetings are called, when circumstances require it. Some churches have no other except *special* church meetings.

V.—Concerts of Prayer.

Quite extensively through the churches the practice prevails of observing the first Monday evening in each month—more commonly now the first Sunday evening—as a concert of prayer for the success and prosperity of missions, and the universal spread of the Gospel. In a similar manner, the second Monday, or Sunday evening, is devoted to special prayer for Sunday schools. There is great advantage in devoting certain times to special prayer for particular objects. The mind becomes better informed respecting such objects, and the heart more deeply interested in their prosperity.

VI.—Female Prayer Meetings.

In many churches are held—and should be in all where practicable- -weekly meetings for prayer by the female members, where mothers offer special and united prayer for their children, wives for their husbands, sisters for their brothers, and all for the prosperity of the church, and the salvation of sinners. Many striking instances of answer to prayer have been witnessed, as the result of such meetings.

VII.—Young People's Meetings.

In many churches, also, a weekly meeting for prayer and conference is held by the young people, for their special profit. At such meetings the young feel, perhaps, less restraint in prayer and exhortation than in other meetings, while the pastor, who should, if possible, attend them, often finds there a better opportunity to give needed cautions and instruction to the young, than other occasions afford. These meetings, however, should never be made an excuse by the young for absenting themselves from, or neglecting to take part in, the other stated meetings of the church.

VIII.—Special Services.

These will, from time to time, occur; such as *Fasts* and *Thanksgiving*, occasions which scarcely differ from ordinary services, except in their special object.

Note 1.—The church, with the concurrence of the pastor, appoints all its meetings.

Note 2.—It is the right and duty of the pastor to conduct all meetings for worship and devotion, and to act as moderator in all meetings for business.

Note 3.—The preaching of the Gospel, the assembling of God's people, prayer and praise, are duties divinely enjoined; but where, when, and under what particular circumstances these shall be done, are incidents to be determined by Christian wisdom and prudence.

Note 4.—A very great mistake is sometimes made by crowding too many services into the Sabbath, thus making it a day of weariness rather than a day of rest. While its sacred hours should not be passed in idleness and inactivity, yet time should be allowed for reflection, reading the Scriptures, private and family devotion, and also for resting the faculties both of body and of mind. Otherwise the design of the Sabbath is not secured.

CHAPTER V.

ITS WORSHIP.

WORSHIP, properly speaking, is adoration, praise, confession, thanksgiving, and supplication, offered up to God. In common language, *worship* means *religious service* in general, and is ordinarily applied to religious services as maintained by Christian churches.

Worship is a most important *duty*, and a most gracious *privilege*. Its influence on individual piety, on the churches' prosperity, and on the general welfare of society, is not sufficiently understood nor valued.

I.—PREACHING.

Preaching, strictly defined, is not worship, though calculated to inspire and aid it. It is addressed to the congregation, rather than to the Deity, and consists of instruction, exhortation, reproof, and warning. It is the most prominent feature of public religious service, and is the principal instrumentality of giving the knowledge of salvation to the world.

1. *The Object of Preaching.*

The true object and design of all Gospel preaching is the salvation of sinners, and the edification of saints. For this purpose our Saviour gave "pastors and teachers, for the perfecting of the saints, for the work of the ministry, for the edifying of the body of Christ;"[1] and thus "warning every man, and teaching every man, in all wisdom, that we may present every man perfect in Christ Jesus."[2] It is not to entertain or recreate an audience, nor to crowd houses with unprofited hearers; nor to build up wealthy or fashionable congregations; nor to teach science, literature, or art; nor to secure temporal prosperity to the church; but to *save souls* by an exhibition of Christ crucified. All preaching which fails of this, fails of its great design and end.

2. *The Character of Preaching.*

All preaching to be profitable should be plain, simple in style, and experimental, practical, and spiritual in matter. All the arts of oratory and the adornments of culture, poorly compensate for the absence of simplicity, earnestness, and spirituality. Nevertheless, with these qualifications,

[1] Eph. iv. 12. [2] Col. i. 28.

the more interesting and acceptable the address and style, the more useful the preaching is likely to be. And each one should "study to show himself approved unto God, a workman that needeth not be ashamed."[1] Many sermons, in themselves really good, are ineffective, because of a dull, uninteresting, or offensive style of expression or manner of address.

3. *The Frequency of Preaching.*

Preaching is not indeed too highly valued as to its *importance*, but it is too much demanded as to its *frequency*. Congregations ordinarily require too much preaching in proportion to the more social services of religion. One sermon on the Sabbath well prepared, well preached, well understood, and well practised, is vastly better than three imperfectly prepared and imperfectly digested. *Two* discourses each Sabbath are all a minister can well preach, or a congregation can profitably hear. And yet, considering the necessities of the world, and that men perish perpetually without the Gospel, the minister should "preach the word; be instant in season and out of season; reprove, rebuke, exhort, with all long-suffering and doctrine."[2]

[1] 2 Tim. ii. 15.

[2] 2 Tim. iv. 2.

NOTE 1.—Whether sermons should be delivered *extemporaneously*, or from *manuscript*, is a question which the preacher must decide. Opinions are divided. The excellency or usefulness of a sermon does not depend on either method. Some subjects cannot be accurately treated without writing. Writing is an important aid, and an invaluable discipline to the preacher. It aids him to think systematically, and express himself concisely and forcibly. But for all ordinary occasions of preaching, it cannot be doubted that an extemporaneous manner of address, is most in accordance with the design of the Gospel, and more agreeable, forcible and profitable to the congregation.

NOTE 2.—Sermons need not of necessity be *read*, even though they be written; nor need the manner of the address be servile and lifeless, even with a manuscript before one. Some men are as free, animated, and vigorous, in preaching from a manuscript, as others are who never wrote a sermon.

II.—PRAYING.[1]

Aside from prayer as a vital element of *individual* Christian life, its importance, as an element of *social* Christian life, is very great. "Ask and it shall be given you; seek, and ye shall find; knock and it shall be opened unto you."[2] There are special blessings promised to *united* prayer, where "if two of you shall agree on earth as touching anything that they shall ask, it shall be done for them of my Father which is in Heaven."[3]

[1] Part First, chap. xv. [2] Matt. vi. 7 [3] Matt. xviii. 19.

1. *The Nature of Prayer.*

Prayer is an address to God, with adoration, confession, supplication, or thanksgiving on behalf of the worshipper, and of other objects of divine clemency. The merits and *intercession of Christ* must evermore be recognized as the only medium of access to, and cause of blessing from the Father. "Whatsoever ye shall ask the Father in my name, he will give it you."[1] The office of the Holy Spirit must also be understood as the only means of communication with the throne of grace: "for we know not what we should pray for as we ought; but the Spirit itself maketh intercession for us, with groanings which cannot be uttered."[2]

2. *Preparation for Prayer.*

There must be a *preparation of heart* in order to lead profitably the devotions of others in addresses to the mercy seat. Not a forethought of words and phrases for that particular prayer, but a knowledge of the nature of prayer, the objects of prayer, and a spirit in harmony with the divine character, and the divine purposes. "He that cometh to God must believe that he is, and that he is a rewarder of them that diligently

[1] John xvi. 23. [2] Rom. viii. 26.

seek him;"[1] "but let him ask in faith, nothing wavering;"[2] "praying in the Holy Ghost."[3] To *make* prayers and to *pray* are very different things. Any one can *make* a prayer who can command the use of language; but to *pray*, the soul must have fellowship with God.

3. *Style of Prayer.*

Prayers should be *simple*, *direct* and *short*. As far as possible, they should express sentiments in which the congregation can unite, and solicit blessings which the congregation needs. They should be *distinctly uttered*, so that others can hear, understand and unite in them, and have nothing in their manner or expression so peculiar as to divert the thoughts of those who hear from the devotion: and "use not vain repetition as the heathen do: for they think that they shall be heard for their much speaking."[4] Beside which, the whole manner and style of address should be solemn and reverential, savoring of meekness and humility, as it is becoming in sinful helpless creatures, when approaching a holy God.

4. *Faults in Prayer.*

The great defect of prayer may be want of

[1] Heb. xi. 6. [2] James i. 6. [3] Jude 20. [4] Matt. vi. 7.

faith, spirituality of mind, and the influences of the Holy Spirit. But there are certain faults in the aim, intention and mode of address, into which the pious sometimes unconsciously fall, which are worthy of attention and correction.

Preaching Prayers, in which Scripture is explained, doctrine expounded, and instruction offered to the congregation.

Exhorting Prayers, where warnings, rebukes, and exhortations, are addressed to individuals, and personal sins pointed out.

Historical Prayers, in which facts and incidents are related, from which inferences and arguments are adduced.

Oratorical Prayers, where special care seems given to the language and manner, as if intended for critical ears.

Complimentary Prayers, in which the excellences of individuals are effectively dwelt on, as if persons were flattered, rather than the Deity addressed.

Fault-finding Prayers, in which the real or fancied faults of the church or of individuals are set forth, existing difficulties mentioned, and advice given, remedies suggested, or rebukes administered.

All such things should be avoided.

III.—Singing.

Singing is a chief part of Christian *worship.* Like prayer, it may express adoration, confession, thanksgiving, supplication and praise. But, unlike prayer, in this act of worship all can vocally unite, "Speaking to themselves in psalms and hymns, and spiritual songs, singing and making melody in their hearts to the Lord."[1]

It is especially adapted to elevate the religious affections—to lighten any load of sorrow that may oppress the heart—to subdue unholy passions—and to harmonize the feelings of those who unite in the exercise. Being performed in concert with others, prevents an unpleasant sense of individual responsibility, and it becomes a pleasant privilege instead of a burdensome duty.

It is the only act of worship in which all occupy a common position and mutually bear a part. It is not, therefore, strange that *singing* occupied so large a place in the religious services of the early Christian churches, or that the gracious affections of the renewed heart cherish it so fondly, and resort to it so frequently.

1. *The Character of Singing.*

It should evidently be the united expression of

[1] Eph. v. 19.

the assembly—the worship of all uttered in song. It is not to be a *performance* for the entertainment of the congregation, but an act of worship *by* the congregation. It is not to be an act of worship performed by others, to which the congregation is to *listen*, but an act of worship which they themselves are to *offer*.

Therefore, singing should be congregational; that is, *the people should sing*—all the assembly should praise God in song. Singing is the *people's worship*. The *chant*, the *anthem*, the *oratorio*, are rather for the cathedral and the temple. Though beautiful and sublime, they should be but incidentally used in the Christian congregation. They inspire worship in the assembly, but the assembly does not to any considerable extent worship in them. The genius of the Gospel and of the Christian sanctuary requires chiefly the *chorus*, where the congregation shall not *listen* and have devotion *excited*, but where they shall *sing* and *express* devotion.

2. *The Style of the Music.*

Since the idea of the Gospel is that *the people shall worship*, not *witness a performance*, therefore the style of the music should be such as the people can perform. But the mass of people can never go beyond the simplest elements of any art or science; therefore, the music of the sanctuary should be of the simplest kind in structure and execution, and limited to a small number of tunes. Music more complicated in structure and more artistic in execution, a few could perform and perhaps more highly enjoy; but it would not express the devotion of the great mass of worshippers, because they could not unite in it. Devotion seeks plain choral harmonies in which to utter its worship.

3. *The Leader of Singing.*

Somebody must lead—that is, decide on the tune and commence the singing. It makes little difference whether the leader be an organ, a single voice, a quartette, or a choir. Either of these would be in accordance with the spirit and design of Christian worship, providing they be simply *leaders*, not *performers.*

If the singing of the sanctuary is to be performed *for* the congregation, and they take no part in it, it matters little whether that performance be by an instrument, a single voice, or several voices. But a Christian congregation should not omit so important a duty, nor deprive itself of so sacred a privilege, as that of singing the praises of God in his house of worship.

NOTE 1.—All *levity* and *irreverence* on the part of choirs and singers, in the house of worship and during the time of religious service, should be strictly and conscientiously avoided. Whispering, studying the music-book, or the hymn-book, and all trifling, are painfully incongruous in scenes of sacred devotion, especially by those who take so prominent a part in worship as do the singers.

NOTE 2.—That *unconverted* and *irreligious persons* may unite in singing divine praise—that they may worship God in song, is evident. Such a course is as appropriate and consistent as for them to pray or read the Scriptures. But for such persons to *do* the *singing* for a Christian congregation, or to *lead* their worship and devotion in song, is as evidently inappropriate and inconsistent as for them to lead their devotions in preaching, prayer, exhortation, or reading the Scriptures.

NOTE 3.—To aid in the better performance of congregational singing, some congregations meet once a week, or at such times as may be convenient, for the purpose of singing over and becoming familiar with hymns and tunes which they may wish to sing on the Sabbath. This is an easy, pleasant, and serviceable means of furthering the design.

NOTE 4.—Every church should provide for the *instruction of the young* connected with the congregation in the elements of sacred music. Such instruction, during six, or at least three months of each year, with a weekly exercise, would soon make congregational singing practicable.

NOTE 5.—Instruction in vocal music should enter largely into the education of all children, both at home and in public and private schools; while in Sabbath-schools a considerable part of the time should be spent in singing. Such a course would prepare the way for better singing, and consequently for better worship in the sanctuary.

IV.—Exhorting.

The gift of *exhortation* is one by which the Spirit edifies and instructs the church. This constitutes a considerable part of the exercise of social religious meetings, where God's people "exhort one another, daily,"[1] and each "suffers the word of exhortation."[2]

There are persons in every Christian congregation, who have a depth and richness of religious experience, and whose remarks are attended with a peculiar unction and power, beyond those of ordinary Christians. This is, doubtless, owing to a closer fellowship and communion with God. But, besides such, *every* Christian disciple can speak of his experience in the divine life, and exhort and encourage others. They are not called to expound scriptures, or hold public meetings, but they can tell of the grace of our Lord Jesus Christ as revealed to them.

The exhortations of God's children form one of the most effectual means of spiritual improvement, and edification to the church. "While he that exhorteth, waits on exhortation."[3]

1. *Who should exhort.*

It is the privilege, and at times, doubtless, the

[1] Heb. iii. 13. [2] Heb. xiii. 22. [3] Rom. xii. 8.

duty, of all who know the grace of God, without distinction of age, sex, or condition, to speak of their experience of that grace, in the meetings for social worship. There, where the freedom which marks "the household of faith" prevails, they should "exhort one another, and so much the more as they see the day approaching."[1]

2. *The Gift of Exhortation.*

By some it is supposed that the *gift* of exhortation is imparted to particular persons, as ministerial gifts are to those called to preach. But every one who speaks from his own experience of the things of godliness, speaks to edification. Ordinary abilities, sanctified by the Spirit, cannot fail to be profitable. Those who speak the most fluently and the most eloquently, do not always speak the most profitably. But those who speak with the Spirit, never fail to edify those who walk in the Spirit.

3. *Faults in Exhortation.*

Christians sometimes fall into faulty habits in this exercise, which hinder their usefulness and mar the spiritual pleasures of social fellowship.

[1] Heb. x. 25.

A preaching style should be avoided, though passages of Scripture will often be mentioned, suggesting trains of reflection of great interest and profit.

Lengthy exhortations should never be indulged in. They deprive others of their privileges, and usually become tedious and irksome, however good in themselves.

One's self should not be too much spoken of, lest it might appear boastful, and egotistic.

Fault-finding and complaining should most carefully be avoided. Few things so effectually close the ears or the hearts of hearers against one, as this.

Denunciation, and a censorious spirit, exhibits a temper so much opposed to the Gospel that harm, and not good, is done by it.

Hobbies are unprofitable. Some always dwell on hackneyed themes, until both themselves and the subjects are unpleasant and distasteful to the audience.

Foreign subjects should not often be introduced, except as illustration, or to draw lessons of instruction from them. Spiritual themes should be those dwelt on in exhortation.

CHAPTER VI.

ITS GOVERNMENT.

THE Christian Church is divinely constituted, and its officers, ordinances, and government are authorized and prescribed either by Christ himself or by the inspiration of his Spirit in the Apostles.

The *government*[1] of a church, according to the New Testament plan, and teaching, is *independent* in form, and the right of administration resides in the body itself. That is, each individual church is entirely independent, and governs itself, manages its own affairs, admits, disciplines, and dismisses its members, and transacts any and all other business necessary to be done, without the aid or interference of any other church or churches. No other individual or body of men whatever, either civil or ecclesiastical, has any authority over it, or right to interfere with its affairs, unless requested so to do.

[1] See Second Part, chap. vi.

That churches have this right of self-government is evident, because Christ in his directions for the treatment of offences, recognizes the church as the ultimate tribunal of appeal, as also its authority to decide finally, cases brought before it. The Apostle in like manner recognizes the right of churches to choose their own officers, and to administer discipline, by enjoining them to do it, reproving them for neglecting it, and commending them for properly performing it.

Both the *right* and the *responsibility* of administering this government Christ has committed to each church. No others can lawfully take these from them, nor can they commit them to any other hands. They cannot transfer the government to the officers, nor to a part of the members, nor to any man or body of men external to the church.

They themselves are accountable to Christ, the Head of the Church, and the King in Zion, for the correct and faithful administration of it.

NOTE 1.—It is, therefore, evident that *all ecclesiastical authority* resides in the *church*; that is, in each individual church. The acts of all other men and bodies of men whatever, are *advisory*, not *authoritative;* inasmuch as the church cannot transfer its authority to them, and Christ has given them no other similar authority.

NOTE 2.—In the administration of its government, and the exercise of its authority, the church is not *legislative* but *execu-*

tive; it cannot *make* laws, but only *execute* those already made by the great Lawgiver. Consequently, it cannot lawfully go beyond the words of Christ, which constitute its law.

NOTE 3.—Each church acts for itself alone, and cannot bind the action of any other church. Each one should, in the spirit of Christian courtesy, respect the action of every other: but only so far as that action is according to the teachings of the New Testament; and every church is to be the judge and interpreter of those teachings for itself.

NOTE 4.—Since the government devolves on the church collectively, constituting a democracy, and because all the individuals composing the body cannot be expected, in all cases, perfectly to harmonize, therefore, it is allowed, that the *majority shall rule.*

NOTE 5.—But *majorities* may err, and do wrong, and their acts transcend the divine statutes, and become unjust and oppressive to *minorities*, thus forming an unlawful adminstration of the government; therefore, the acts of majorities are only to be recognized, approved, and sanctioned, when they are evidently in accordance with the laws of Christ as recorded in the New Testament.

NOTE 6.—In disputes and differences of opinions, large minorities are, perhaps, quite as likely to be right, as small majorities, therefore, majorities should act cautiously, and not invade their rights. But if minorities think themselves injured, there is no source of redress, no higher tribunal of appeal. They may retire, and find a home in some other church. Or they may organize themselves into a new one. Or they may call a council, and receive advice and an expression of opinions. But a council can neither correct the wrong, nor punish the wrong-doers, any further than the force of their advice and opinions may affect them, or the public sentiment.

NOTE 7.—By many it is thought an evil in the independent form of church government, and a defect in its democratic constitution, that there is no central and ultimate tribu nal of appeal beyond and above the individual church, where both churches and ministers, when unfaithful and unworthy, can be judged and punished. But this evil is more apparent than real. And so far as the system *is* subject to abuse, the evils are abundantly compensated by the real, substantial and important advantages which it secures.

Indeed it is enough to say that this form and method of government is *divinely given;* therefore, it must be right. Therefore, also, it must be liable to the fewest evils, and productive of the greatest benefits.

NOTE 8.—Though one church cannot exercise any act of discipline upon another, yet one may pass an act of *disfellowship* against another, for sufficient cause. Such an act is merely an expression of disapproval of, and refusal to, hold fellowship with said church in the communion of the Supper, for the reasons stated. An act of disfellowship, however, is seldom called for, and should be resorted to only for very grave causes, such as evident departures from the faith of the Gospel, either in its teachings or its practices, and which departures make it unworthy the confidence of sister churches. When done from trifling causes, such as differences in mere matters of internal order and discipline, it results more to the prejudice of those disfellowshipping, than of those disfellowshipped.

CHAPTER VII.

ITS MINISTRY.

THE *Gospel Ministry* is of divine appointment, and stands first and highest among the instrumentalities of spiritual good to the world. Whatever other agencies there may be for spreading the truth, whether religious *education*, the religious *press*, or any other, still the *ministry* is foremost, since that is specially ordained of Christ.

The *ministry* is appointed to instruct and edify the church, and to bear the knowledge of salvation to the world. Every Christian disciple is under obligation to do this to the extent of his ability; but in order that there should be no failure in this work, Christ ordained that a particular class and profession of men should be appointed to the work, whose special and exclusive duty it should be to preach the Gospel.

Our Saviour "ordained twelve that they should be with him, and that he might send them forth to preach;"[1] and "after these things the Lord appointed other seventy also, and sent

[1] Mark iii. 14.

them two and two before his face."[1] And his instructions were, "Go ye, therefore, and teach all nations, baptizing them in the name of the Father, and of the Son, and of the Holy Ghost; teaching them to observe all things whatsoever I have commanded you; and lo, I am with you alway, even unto the end of the world. Amen."[2]

I.—A Call to the Ministry.

A *divine call* to the work of the Gospel ministry is, and must ever be, insisted on by Christian churches, if the spirituality of religion is to be maintained.

It is not enough that a man has piety, and talent, and education, and ability to explain the Scriptures, and a facility in addressing congregations, and an earnest desire to do good, in order to enter this sacred office. It must not be the mere choice of a profession, nor the dictate of an ambition, which looks to the pulpit as a place for achieving distinction.

It must not be in obedience to the opinions or persuasions of friends. "No man taketh this honor unto himself, but he that is called of God."[3] He that would lawfully enter the Gospel ministry must do it from the deep, undoubted, and unalterable conviction, wrought into the

[1] Luke x. 1. [2] Matt. xxviii. 19. [3] Heb. v. 4.

heart by the Holy Spirit, that such is the will and good pleasure of God concerning him—that this, and nothing else, is the work of life, appointed by God for him, whether it may bring joy or sorrow, honor or dishonor, prosperity or adversity. He that can follow any other profession or business with a peaceful mind, and a conscience void of offence toward God, should never enter the ministry.

The *signs* and *evidences* of a divine call to the work of the ministry, are various. One evidence, and the greatest, is the inward teaching of the Spirit, by which, after long, deliberate, and prayerful consideration, and perhaps painful conflict, the conviction becomes deep and permanent in the mind, that to preach the Gospel is the work which God has assigned to him. Another sign is, that the mind is led, by the Spirit, into a fruitful contemplation of the Scriptures, whose spirit and meaning, whose rich and gracious treasures, are unfolded and made plain to an unusual degree.

An increasing facility of expression, a freedom of utterance, when attempting to explain, enforce, or illustrate any particular passage of Scripture, in public meetings, is a further indication of a call to the ministry. Though at times all this may be reversed in one's experience, and but little freedom of thought or of utterance be enjoyed, yet if, on the whole, there is an increasing capability, it may be regarded as evidence of the divine intention. Still further, if there be a divine call, there will be a corresponding conviction on the part of the pious and prayerful people of God. They will be interested in, and spiritually profited by, the exercise of such gifts, and they will at length be convinced that such a one is called to preach the Gospel.

And more still, if God has called one to preach, he will, in his providence, open ways for him to pursue that course of duty. There may be many difficulties in the way. The young man, who has some conviction that he is called to this work, should not be impatient nor too hasty. It may require long months to settle that question satisfactorily. Let him wait, and carefully observe the indications of providence and the directions of the Spirit. Let him improve every opportunity that opens before him, but not attempt to hasten providences. Let him improve his gifts as occasion offers, and sooner or later he will become satisfied, as will also his brethren, whether or not he is called to preach.

NOTE 1.—It is no part of a call to the ministry that the heart rises in persistent opposition, and obstinately rebels against the divine indication. Some almost suppose that in order to have a satisfactory evidence of a divine call they must stoutly resist the will of God. This is a great mistake. Such opposition and unwillingness may arise from a deep conviction of one's unfitness for the work, or more frequently, from the prospect of sacrificing the objects of a generous ambition in worldly goods and gains, for that life of self-denial and toil which is the lot of a faithful minister.

NOTE 2.—Another mistake should be guarded against. A young man may be ambitious of distinction in the world, and suppose that the pulpit is the best field for ability and learning to secure that result. The pulpit will prove the most difficult and disastrous of all positions to one whom God has not called into it.

NOTE 3.—Young men exercised on this question should avoid the influence of Christian friends in *two* respects. *First*, they should not be too much affected by the encouragements of those ardent and over partial, whose sympathies are warm and impulsive, but whose discernment may not be great, and whose judgment would not be a safe guide. *Second*, they should not be too much discouraged by any apparent indifference, or neglect which they may seem to receive from members of the church, or Christian friends generally. All these things are to be carefully weighed, but each one for himself, must ultimately be judge in the matter, and act from his own, rather than from the convictions of others

II.—THE PERPETUITY OF MINISTERIAL OBLIGATIONS.

Is the obligation involved in a divine call and appointment to the work of the Gospel ministry, of perpetual force? Or may a man called to that work, leave it at any time for some other business, or calling?

It is admitted on all hands, by evangelical Christians, that such a call is of *perpetual obligation*. It is evident that if God has put one into the ministry, the same divine authority is requisite to direct, or give permission to leave it and enter upon some other work. If disabled from the work, or hindered in it by providences which he cannot control, this may be regarded as an indication of the divine will, that he may remit the work permanently, or temporarily, as the indications may be. But no young man should enter the ministry with any other idea than that it is for life. How one who believes himself called of God to preach the Gospel can, quietly and conscientiously, devote himself to other business and pursuits, without such providential compulsion it is difficult to understand.

III.—The Sphere of Ministerial Labor.

The pastor's special and particular field of labor is in his own church and congregation, for the spiritual good of the people. He should, indeed, do all he can to countenance and aid every good cause and undertaking, by all consistent means but in no way that shall prevent or hinder a full and faithful discharge of his duties to his own flock, where his first and principal duties call him. Ministers should, therefore, and especially "take heed unto themselves, and to all the flock, over which the Holy Ghost hath made them overseers, to feed the church of God, which he hath purchased with his own blood."[1]

It must also be observed, that in many places the pastor is compelled to devote a portion of his time to secular pursuits, in order to meet the necessities of life, and support himself and family. But this should be done for *godliness*, not for *gain*; as a means to enable him to preach the Gospel, not for worldly profit. This expedient, which is commendable under the circumstances, should be abandoned, and his whole time and energy devoted to the ministry, so soon as he can be comfortably supported by the people.

IV.—The Source of Ministerial Authority.

Whence does the minister of the Gospel derive his authority to preach and to administer the ordinances? Not from the *Church*, for they have no such authority to give. Not from a *Council*, since councils possess no ecclesiastical authority, being *advisory* only. Not from the *State*, for the state, as such, has no right of interference,

[1] Acts xx. 28.

either for authority or advice in ecclesiastical affairs. His authority, then, is derived from *no human source*, but from *Christ*, the great Head of the church, directly, by the witness and endowment of the Holy Spirit. No one can be correctly called, "but he that is called of God, as was Aaron."[1]

All that a church or a council can rightfully do is to express their approbation or disapprobation of a man's entering the ministry. The force of *ordination* is simply a recognition, an approbation and sanction, in a public and an impressive manner, of what is believed to be the divine appointment of the candidate to the work of the ministry. The object of council and of church action is, not to impart the right or ability to preach the Gospel, but to ascertain if such right and ability have been divinely imparted, and if so, to approve their exercise. Ministerial rights and abilities are not subject to councils, nor to churches; but churches and councils judge of their existence, and approve of their exercise.[2]

NOTE 1.—Any individual who believes himself called of God to the work, as one under law to Christ, and ultimately responsible to him alone, has a right to preach the Gospel, though churches and councils, should oppose such a course.

[1] Heb. v. 4.

[2] See Part First, chap. xii. 1.

NOTE 2.—The right of any man to be the minister and pastor of any particular church, is derived from that *church* itself. No man, or body of men can make him a minister to *them* without their consent; while, if they so determine and choose him, he is to them a minister, though councils and churches should forbid it. A man's authority to preach the Gospel and administer the ordinances comes from God directly, and only. A man's right to do these things in any particular church, comes from that church alone.

NOTE 3.—But suppose a man believes himself called to preach, and insists on the exercise of this right, while the church of which he is a member, after long and careful consideration, are convinced that he has not been called to that work, and that he ought not to undertake it. The church has its *authority*, as well as the individual his *rights*. In such a case, the church may, in the exercise of its lawful and legitimate authority, labor with, admonish, and if need be, rebuke such a one, and if he will not hear them, discipline and even exclude him from its fellowship, if such a course be deemed necessary.

V.—THE ORDINATION OF MINISTERS.

The New Testament meaning of *ordination* is "appointing," "setting apart" to the ministerial work—one who was divinely called to it. In the case of a pastor, the appointment, or ordination was done by a vote of the church; in the case of an evangelist or missionary by the concurrent agreement of the church and ministers interested. Thus our Saviour "ordained twelve that they should be with him,"[1] and "appointed

[1] Mark iii. 14.

other seventy, also,"[1] and Paul directed Titus to "ordain elders in every city."[2]

This ordination, or appointment, was sometimes, perhaps usually, accompanied by prayer for the divine blessing, and by the laying on of hands by the *Presbytery*, that is the presbyters, or ministers, as a solemn dedication of the individual to a most sacred and responsible work.

Ordination, therefore, as now practised, does not pretend to confer any authority, rights, abilities, or power on the candidate, either by churches or councils, but in a formal and solemn manner, to recognize him as one whom God has called, and the church has chosen to the work of the ministry, and to give him the sanction and encouragement of their approbation in it. Some public religious service is usually held, though not essential, nor is the particular form of it prescribed by any Scriptural precept or example, except as prayer and the laying on of hands, has the warrant of Apostolical precedent.

The usual course of proceeding is as follows: The church of which the candidate is a member, having determined on his ordination, invites a council by sending letters to such churches as they prefer, requesting them to send their pastor

[1] Luke x. 1. [2] Tit. i. 5.

and brethren (usually two) to consider the propriety of, and if the candidate should be approved, to aid in ordaining. In some parts it is customary, instead of a council, to call the ministers only. The council, when convened, examines the candidate as to his "Christian experience," "Call to the ministry," and "Views of Scripture doctrine." If satisfied in all these respects, they vote their approval, and proceed to the services of ordination, either at the same, or at some subsequent time, as the council shall decide. It is customary to appoint ministers to perform various parts, such as the "sermon," "ordaining prayer," "hand of fellowship," "charge to the candidate," and, if ordained as a pastor, "charge to the church." In these appointments the candidate is usually consulted.

NOTE 1.—If the council should refuse to ordain the candidate, still the church can have him as their minister if they choose to do so, and none can prevent them. The independence of churches cannot be questioned. This, however, under ordinary circumstances, would not be expedient. Neither the church nor candidate would be likely to command the approbation, respect, and confidence of the churches, or the community at large, after a council had refused to ordain, for what it considered good cause.[1]

NOTE 2.—A call to the ministry does not of necessity involve

[1] See Part First, chap. xii. 1.

an immediate entrance upon its duties. Hence, a church or a council may have good reason to believe that a young man has been called to the work, and yet, on account of his inexperience, want of knowledge of church structure and discipline, and of ministerial duties, or for other reasons, may think it highly important that he should be instructed in the ways of the Lord more perfectly, before assuming the government of the church, and the public duties of the ministry; in the meantime improving his gifts in more private spheres.

NOTE 3.—Since the peace and prosperity of a church so vitally depends on the knowledge, discretion, and experience of a pastor, and his ability to guide its affairs, as well as his ability to preach the Gospel, therefore a church should use the utmost care in calling one to ordination, and the council which examines him, should give a wide range to their investigations, and thoroughly inquire into his general competency for the work.

VI.—THE QUALIFICATIONS OF MINISTERS.

The qualifications of Gospel ministers, as prescribed by inspiration, are set forth in the pastoral Epistles of Paul, and should be earnestly insisted on by churches and councils. They are found in 1 Tim., chap. iii., and in Titus, chap. i., as follows:

He should be "blameless," "the husband of one wife," "vigilant," "sober," "of good behavior," "given to hospitality," "apt to teach," "not given to wine," "no striker," "not greedy of filthy lucre," "patient," "not a brawler," "not covetous," "one that ruleth well his own house, having his children in subjection," "not a novice," "bearing a good report of them that are without," "not self-willed," "not soon angry." Such qualifications could not fail to make good ministers of Jesus Christ.

NOTE 1.—As to a course of *scholastic education*, whether literary or theological, as a preparation for the work of the ministry, no certain amount nor given standard can be fixed upon. The importance and difficulties of the ministerial profession make it necessary that the student should avail himself of the largest and most liberal culture practicable under the circumstances. His own convictions of duty, the indications of Providence, and the advice of wise and prudent friends, must decide the question. Certain it is, that no given amount of preparatory study is an indispensable condition of ministerial fitness, or of ministerial success.

NOTE 2.—By the student in his preparatory study, a prudent discretion is to be used as to the exercise of his ministerial gifts. It is of the greatest advantage to him that he often engage in preaching and other religious duties in public. But this should not be pursued to such an extent as to become injurious, by diverting his mind from study, and preventing that mental training and acquisition of knowledge so important for him to possess.

VII.—THE DISCIPLINE OF MINISTERS.

Ministers, as members of the church, are subject to its authority and discipline, the same as other members. But since, from the nature of their office and standing, their course and conduct may affect the interests of Gospel truth more widely than that of private members, it requires unusual wisdom and prudence in dealing with them, when they fall into error and sin. For the same reason unfavorable reports respecting them should be received with great caution, and charges which implicate their moral, or ministerial character, should be entertained only on very strong evidence. Thus the Apostle justly and prudently decreed, "Against an elder receive not an accusation, but before two or three witnesses."[1]

In instances of discipline, where the case is clear, the church proceeds accordingly. If the case be doubtful and difficult, and the church divided in counsel and action, it will be judicious to call in private brethren as advisers, or to call a council for advice, and add the sanction of their opinions to the action of the church. Such decisions will seem less the result of passion or of prejudice, than the judgment, of an agitated church.

NOTE 1.—A council can neither make nor unmake a minister. No council, therefore, can put a man out of the ministry. All they can do, is to declare that he is, in their opinion, unfit or disqualified to be a minister, and that they cannot fellowship him as such.

NOTE 2.—All ecclesiastical authority resides in a *church*, and yet a church cannot, in any proper and absolute sense, *depose*

[1] 1 Tim. v. 19.

a man from the ministry, except so far as that ministry relates to themselves. They can discharge or depose him from being *their* minister, and declare him, in their opinion, unworthy to fill the sacred office. But any other church can have him as *their* minister, if they so desire, since each church is entirely independent in the choice of its own officers.

NOTE 3.—Such action, however, on the part of councils or churches, though having no power to compel or to enforce penalties, substantially effects the same end through the force of public sentiment, which will, sooner or later, lead a man thus declared unworthy, to retire from the sacred calling.

NOTE 4.—A church might declare a man unfit for the ministry, and discharge him from its office, while, at the same time, they might be satisfied to retain him still in their fellowship, as a private member. His *ministerial*, rather than his *Christian* character being involved in the discipline.

NOTE 5.—If a minister be *excluded* from the fellowship of a church, such exclusion is a deposition from the ministry, so far as any church action can effect a deposition. If a man be not fit to be a member of a church, he cannot be fit to be a minister of the Gospel.

VIII.—THE LICENSING OF MINISTERS.[1]

It is customary for churches to grant a *license* to those whom they believed called to preach, but who are not yet ready for ordination, and a full entrance upon the work of the ministry. This license is simply an approval by the church of the course which the candidate is pursuing. It imparts no rights, and confers no powers upon

[1] See Second Part, chap. viii. 11.

the candidate, but only expresses the conviction that he possesses gifts and capabilities which indicate a call to the ministry.

A license should not be given by the church until they have had sufficient opportunity to judge for themselves in the case. Churches should be exceedingly careful not to grant licenses without sufficient evidence of a *divine call* in the case of the candidate, and equally careful to approve and encourage, where there is good evidence of such a call.

NOTE 1.—Ordination does not, of necessity, follow the granting of a *license*. The *church may have occasion* to change their opinion of the candidate's call, and may, at any time, for sufficient cause, *revoke* his license.

NOTE 2.—A church should never grant a license as a matter of mere gratification or convenience, or simply because they dislike to refuse.

NOTE 3.—A *letter of commendation* is sometimes given a young man, approving of his entering upon a course of study, with the ministry in view, but deferring the *license* until better opportunities are offered to judge of his gifts and calling.

CHAPTER VIII.

ITS MEMBERSHIP.

THE nature of *Church Membership* is a question of great importance. What are the *qualifications* for, *rights* and *privileges* of members; how the relation may be formed, and how it can be dissolved; all these are questions vital to a scriptural church polity, and to each member's welfare.

I.—QUALIFICATIONS FOR MEMBERSHIP.

The *qualifications* for church membership are *three*, namely:

1. *A Regenerate Heart.*—The person must be able to give satisfactory evidence that he has been regenerated by the Spirit of God, and has passed from death to life.

2. *A Scriptural Faith.*—He should also in the judgment of the church, have his faith based on, and according to the Scriptures, so as not to bring false doctrines into the body of Christ.

3. *A Christian Life.*—His life, since he has professed faith in Christ, must be consistent with

that profession, and according to godliness so far as it is, or can be known by the church.

NOTE 1.—It is not every person that can give an equally satisfactory relation of Christian experience; nor are those always the most certainly regenerate, who can tell the most remarkable experience. But no person should be admitted, unless the church, in some way, have satisfactory evidence that he is regenerate.

NOTE 2.—Persons on entering a church may be *ignorant* of many things in Scripture doctrine, which they will afterwards learn. Nor should they be rejected simply on that account. Indeed, they enter the church as the school of Christ, to receive instruction. But no one should be admitted who holds and maintains doctrines *contrary* to the Scriptures.

II.—MODE OF ADMISSION.

There are *three* ways in which a person may be admitted to membership in the church:

1. *By Baptism.*—A person may be admitted by baptism, on a profession of faith in Christ. Such a one makes known his desire for baptism to the pastor, or brethren, who become satisfied of his fitness for membership.

Then the person, if encouraged by the pastor and brethren, comes before the church at its church meeting, or such other time as it may appoint, and relates his Christian experience, and views of duty and of doctrine. After he has retired, the church votes whether he shall be received to membership "*on being baptized.*"

In some churches, the name of the candidate is announced at a public meeting, previous to that on which he is to be received, to give all an opportunity of acquaintance with the fact. In some churches also, the candidate is required to come before a committee and make his request; and if the committee regard it unfavorably, his application is not presented to the church at all.

2. *By Letter.*—A person may receive from the church, of which he is already a member, a letter of commendation and dismission, and with it be received to membership in another church, providing the one from which he comes be of the same faith and order.

Such a one is received by vote of the church, as in the previous case; and though not absolutely necessary, yet it is desirable that he should be present, and verbally express his wish to be received.

3. *By Experience.*—It is sometimes the case, that persons who have received baptism, but by some means are not members of any church, or are members in another denomination, desire to be admitted to membership. They bring no letters, nor are they re-baptized; but after giving a satisfactory relation of their Christian experi-

ence, and if their faith and Christian character be satisfactory, they are admitted to the fellowship of the church *on their Christian experience.*

The names of candidates to be received by *letter* and *experience*, as well as those for baptism, are publicly announced at some meeting previous to their reception.

Note *a.*—In many churches, particularly in cities and large towns, to guard as carefully as possible against receiving unsuitable persons, some member named by the pastor acts as a committee to inquire into the case of each one to be received, and reports to the church at the time of his reception.

Note 1.—Persons cannot be received to membership on the credit of *letters*, from other denominations. Such letters are accepted only as testimonials of their previous standing and Christian character; but the applicants are to be received either by *baptism*—if not already baptized—or on their Christian *experience*, related in person before the church.

Note 2.—It is a rule, generally acted on, that no person shall be received into the church to the grief of any one who is already a member. Hence, although the vote of a majority present at any regular meeting properly decides any question of business, yet, in receiving and excluding members, and other important business, it is very desirable there should be a general harmony, and if possible, entire unanimity.

Note 3.—It may often be expedient for the church to postpone the reception of a candidate, for a time, to give opportunity for a better acquaintance with him, and for greater harmony in its action respecting him. But the Scriptures certainly do not authorize any system of *probation*, by which every candidate is required to wait a specified time, before being admitted to the fellowship of the church.

NOTE 4.—To baptize persons who *do not unite with any church*, is generally considered subversive of good order, and destructive of church organization. They should be approved of, and received by the church, before being baptized. Yet there are possible exceptions, where no church exists, or where they are baptized to constitute one, and in some other unusual and extraordinary circumstances.

NOTE 5.—Nor is it expedient or promotive of good order, for ministers to baptize persons, who wish to unite with churches of another denomination. Such persons should receive baptism from the pastors of the churches with which they unite.

NOTE 6.—Persons who give evidence of a regenerate heart, a scriptural faith, and a godly life, *have a right* to be admitted to the privileges of the church, and are not to be denied baptism and membership, if they request it.

NOTE 7.—It is customary, when members are admitted to the church, whether by letter or baptism, for the pastor to give them "*the right hand of fellowship.*" This is usually done at the communion service, immediately before the ordinance is administered. The act is designed, simply as an expression of the church's welcome and fellowship for those received; and though not required by any scriptural authority, is very appropriate, and is favored by Scripture analogy. In some churches, particularly at the South, the hand of fellowship is given by the various members present, in order, instead of by the pastor exclusively; a practice which, though less convenient, is a more forcible expression of fraternal welcome.

III.—MODE OF DISMISSION.

There are also *three* ways of dismissing members from the church.

1. *By Letter.*[1]—A member may receive a let-

[1] See Second Part, chap. viii. i. 8.

ter of commendation and dismission from the church of which he is a member, and with it unite with another church of the same faith; and when so united is dismissed from the former church.

2. *By Exclusion.*—When the church, in the exercise of its lawful discipline, withdraws the hand of fellowship from any one, he is thenceforth no longer a member.

3. *By Death.*—The death of members, of course, dissolves their connection with the church on earth.

NOTE 1.—No member can *withdraw* from the church. He must be regularly dismissed by the action of the church. Nor can one have his name *dropped*, nor be *excluded*, at his own request.

NOTE 2.—Nor can the church *compel* any one *to take a letter* and withdraw, without his consent. Such would be virtually an *exclusion* from its fellowship.

NOTE 3.—The one receiving a letter, *is still a member*, and subject to the authority and discipline of that church, until he has actually connected himself with another.

NOTE 4.—It is usual for the validity of letters to be *limited* to some specified time—three, six, or twelve months; after the expiration of which time they are useless, but may be renewed.

NOTE 5.—Letters thus given, *can be revoked* by the church at its discretion, any time previous to their being used.

NOTE 6.—Any member has a *right*, at any time, to ask for, and receive from the church, a *certificate* of his membership and standing; but subjects himself to discipline, if he makes an improper use of it.

NOTE 7.—Letters cannot properly be given to unite with a church of another denomination. It would be manifestly inconsistent for one church to dismiss or recommend its members to unite with another church with which it did not hold fellowship.

NOTE 8.—If members have occasion to remove their residence near some other church of the same faith and order, they should take letters and unite where they go. Churches should require their members to do this, unless the circumstances are so peculiar as to make it impracticable. The too common practice of holding membership in one church, and habitually worshipping with another, cannot be justified, nor approved.

NOTE 9.—Persons *excluded* from one church, should not be received to the fellowship of another, except where the most manifest wrong has been done them, and where the church excluding, refuses to do them justice; nor even then, till after the most patient and careful investigation, and endeavors to reconcile the difficulty. Yet cases may occur, where it is the duty of one church to bear this witness against the manifest wrong done by another, and to receive the unjustly excluded member into its own fellowship.

NOTE 10.—When a member unites with a church of another denomination, *the hand of fellowship is withdrawn from him*, though otherwise of good Christian character, and though he may have acted conscientiously in what he has done. The act implies no immorality, but as his church is not in fellowship with that to which he has gone, they cannot consistently continue fellowship with him in such a church.

NOTE 11.—In voting on the reception, dismission, discipline, or exclusion of members, several cases should not be included in the same vote, but *each one* acted on singly and separately.

NOTE 12.—The *dropping* of members is merely placing on a separate list the names of those of whom the church has lost all knowledge. They are not dismissed from the church, nor reported as members; but whenever discovered their names are restored to the record. No one can be *dropped* as an act of *discipline*, nor when his residence is known.

CHAPTER IX.

ITS DISCIPLINE.

By *discipline* is meant that system of internal order and government by which the church administers the laws of Christ, so as best to secure the peace, purity, edification, and efficiency of each member and of the whole body. It applies particularly to the settlement of difficulties, and the removal of offences—what is sometimes called *corrective discipline.*

It is of the utmost importance that a correct Scriptural discipline be strictly maintained in every church. The neglect of it fills a church with evils which check the growth of piety, hinder the success of the Gospel, and reproach the Christian profession; while from an injudicious, unreasonable, and unscriptural exercise of it, more difficulties, dissensions, and divisions have arisen than perhaps from any other single cause.

Every well organized society or government has its laws and regulations, in which each one on becoming a member or citizen, acquiesces, to which he pledges his support, and by which he submits to be governed, so long as he shall belong to it, and leave it, if he ever leaves it, according to its stipulated forms. A Christian church is the most perfectly constructed society known to men, and its system of government and discipline, the most complete. As each member, on entering a church, solemnly covenants to maintain and observe these, so he should consider himself bound by the most sacred responsibilities to honor and observe its doctrines, ordinances, and regulations, so long as he shall remain in it.

There are *three laws* for Christ's house, royal decrees, given by him who is "Head over all things to the Church,"[1] which stand invested with all the sanctions of divine authority, and which, could they be known, loved, and obeyed, if they did not absolutely prevent all offences, would obviate the necessity for private labor and public discipline. They would make churches "households of faith," where Christians should abide "in the unity of the spirit, and in the bond of peace;"[2] green pastures where the flock should rest in safety, and feed with joy. Will not every disciple make them the guide of his life?

[1] Eph. i. 22. [2] Eph. iv. 3.

First law: for every disciple; the law of love.—"A new commandment I give unto you, that ye love one another; as I have loved you, that ye also love one another."[1] This, if strictly obeyed, would prevent all cause of grief and offence, either personally to brethren, or publicly to the church. It would prevent cold indifference to each other's welfare, unfounded suspicions, causeless accusations, jealousies, animosities, bitterness, hatred, and revenge, and cause each to love the other "with a pure heart, fervently."

Second law: for the offender; the law of confession.—"If thou bring thy gift to the altar, and there rememberest that thy brother hath aught against thee, leave there thy gift before the altar, and go thy way; first be reconciled to thy brother, and then come and offer thy gift."[2] This law makes it obligatory on every one who supposes that a brother has aught against him, to go to such a one without delay, and procure a reconciliation. And this he must do, whether there is any just cause or not for that brother to have aught against him. Whether or not he has given that brother reason for grief; but knowing that he has grief, he must go and attempt a reconciliation with him.

[1] John xiii. 34. [2] Matt. v. 23

Third law: for the offended; the law of forgiveness.—"If thy brother trespass against thee rebuke him: and if he repent, forgive him. And if he trespass against thee seven times in a day, and seven times in a day turn to thee saying, I repent, thou shalt forgive him."[1] This enjoins a perpetual personal forgiveness of injuries. It does not indeed require the same regard for one after repeated offences, as before; for this might be impossible. Nor does it require that a church should of necessity be hindered from undertaking a course of discipline with an offender, nor prevented from completing a course already begun, simply because he declares his repentance.

Unhappily these laws are not strictly observed, because offences do come. It is needful, therefore, that each one should understand how to deal with them.

1. The *object* of discipline is to encourage and increase the good, and to restrain, rebuke, and remove the evil, "for the edifying of the body of Christ," that it may be "perfect in love," and without reproach. It is not to gratify personal animosities, nor to secure selfish ends, but to reclaim the wandering, guide the wayward, and

[1] Luke xvii. 3.

secure the best spiritual welfare of each and of all for which discipline is to be exercised.

2. The *spirit* of discipline, in which it must be administered in order to be effective, is of the very first importance. It must not be a spirit of dictation, of pride, of vindictiveness, nor of assumed superiority, but of gentleness, meekness and love. The perpetual guide, worthy to be written in gold on the walls of every church, or better still, inscribed by the Spirit of God in every Christian heart, is "Brethren, if a man be overtaken in a fault, ye which are spiritual, restore such a one in the spirit of meekness."[1]

3. The *right* of discipline cannot be questioned. That churches have a right to exercise a constant watch-care over all their members, to reprove them when erring, and withdraw fellowship from them when incorrigible, is a necessity arising from the very nature of their organization, and is most clearly declared by our Saviour, and recognized by his Apostles. "But if he neglect to hear the church, let him be unto thee as a heathen man and a publican;"[2] "Therefore put away from among yourselves that wicked person."[3]

4. The *duty* of discipline is evident from the

[1] Gal. vi. 2. [2] Matt. xviii. 17. [3] 1 Cor. v. 13.

consideration of its nature, its objects, and the right to exercise it with which the church is invested. A church is unfaithful to itself, and to Christ, and to each of its members, which neglects it. "If thy brother trespass against thee rebuke him; and if he repent forgive him."[1] "Them that sin, rebuke before all, that others also may fear."[2] "Wherefore come out from among them."[3] Because if "one member suffer, all the members suffer with it."[4]

5. The *limit* of discipline is the law of Christ. The church cannot go beyond what the Scriptures authorize; it cannot *make* laws—it can only execute those which Christ has made. It must not invent rules or plans of government, but only use those found in the word of God. "I beseech you, brethren, mark them which cause divisions and offences, contrary to the doctrine which ye have learned."[5] "Now I praise you, brethren, that ye remember me in all things, and keep the ordinances as I delivered them to you."[6]

6. The *result* of discipline—of all corrective discipline—must be the correction or removal of the evil—the reclamation or expulsion of the evil doer. A course of discipline begun for the

[1] Luke xvii. 3. [2] 1 Tim. v. 20. [3] 2 Cor. vi. 18.
[4] 1 Cor. xii. 26. [5] Rom. xvi. 17. [6] 1 Cor. xi. 2.

correction of offences, must not cease until one of these results be secured. "Now we command you, brethren, in the name of our Lord Jesus Christ, that ye withdraw yourselves from every brother that walketh disorderly, and not after the tradition which he received of us."[1] "If he neglect to hear the church, let him be unto thee as a heathen man and a publican."[2]

Offences are usually considered as of *two* kinds: namely, *private* and *public*. These terms are not designed to express the nature or degree of evil done, nor are these classes very clearly defined. This distinction has reference mainly to the objects of offences, and the manner of their treatment.

I.—Private Offences.

A *private offence* is an offence committed by one member against another member, and not against the whole church, as such. It is an injury done by word, action, or otherwise, intentionally or unintentionally, by one member, against the person, character, estate, or feelings, of another member.

So long as such matters of difficulty exist and are treated privately; that is, between the per-

[1] 2 Thes. iii. 6. [2] Matt. xviii. 17.

sons concerned, and are not brought before the church in a public manner for its notice and action, they are *private* offences; but become *public* when brought before the church.

The course to be pursued in such a case, is prescribed by our Saviour in Matthew xviii. Any departure from this rule, is in itself an offence. It is as follows:

1. *First Step.*—The member who considers himself *injured*, must go to the *offending one*, tell him his cause of grief, and between themselves alone, if possible, adjust and settle the difficulty. "If thy brother shall trespass against thee, go and tell him his fault between thee and him alone; if he shall hear thee, thou hast gained thy brother."

NOTE 1.—It is here made obligatory on the *injured* or offended one to go to the offender. This is wisely ordained, since, although the offender is bound by every consideration of justice to go to the offended brother, and confess his sin, yet possibly he may not be aware of the evil he has done, or he may be so perverse and evil-minded as to be unwilling to do justice to an injured brother. But the offended one having done no wrong himself, would be likely to go in a gentle, meek, and forgiving temper of mind, prepared to "gain a brother."

NOTE 2.—This rule requires that the offended member shall go and tell the offender his fault between themselves *alone*. No fear, or false delicacy, shall prevent his telling him his fault. He must not tell it to *any one else*, until he has told the offender.

He must not tell it in the presence of any third person. His object must be to "gain his brother," not to accuse, condemn, or punish him. Nor must he say that since the other did the wrong, he must come to him first.

2. *Second Step.*—If this step shall fail of success, then the *offended* member must take one or two of the brethren, seek another interview with the *offender*, and thus, possibly, by their united wisdom and piety, they may succeed, where himself alone had failed. "But if he will not hear thee, then take with thee one or two more, that in the mouth of two or three witnesses every word may be established."

NOTE 3.—The offended one must not make the matter public even after the first attempt at reconciliation; nor abandon the matter, unless, indeed, he has "gained his brother;" nor tell it to any except to the "one or two more."

NOTE 4.—The object of taking the "one or two more," (who should be pious, prudent, and experienced brethren,) is chiefly that they may act as witnesses between the two. They shall witness whether the offended brother goes in the right spirit; whether he has sufficient ground for complaint; whether he has evidence to sustain his charge; and, also, whether the offender exhibits a wrong spirit. Thus will they be prepared to testify in the case if it comes before the church, so that the church can have their testimony on which to base their own action. This "one or two more" are also to act as mediators between the offender and the offended, and if possible settle the difficulty.

3. *Third Step.*—If this attempt also be unsuc-

cessful, then the *injured* one must tell the whole matter to the *church*, and leave it in their hands to be disposed of as they shall think best. "And if he shall neglect to hear them, tell it unto the church; and if he neglect to hear the church, let him be unto thee as a heathen man, and a publican."

NOTE 5.—When he refuses to hear the "one or two more," then it is to be told to the church, and not till then. It then becoming a public offence, is in the hands of the church to be disposed of, as in their wisdom they shall think best.

NOTE 6.—Let it be here observed that a mere *neglect* to hear the "one or two more" brings it before the church; and a *neglect* to hear the church, ends in exclusion. An open and decided refusal to hear the church, is not necessary; but only a neglect to hear, persisted in by the offender.

It should be most solemnly impressed on the mind of every church member and every church officer, that this course, for the treatment of personal difficulties, was prescribed by Christ as a positive law for his church, and that it stands invested with all the sanctions of divine authority, and can never be departed from with impunity. If every church would require a strict and invariable compliance with this course of procedure, it would greatly lessen the number of personal difficulties, and make those which did arise comparatively harmless.

NOTE 7.—All this is to be done in love and meekness—in the spirit of Christ, with the desire and manifest design to win an erring brother, rather than to be avenged on, and to punish an offending member.

NOTE 8.—Every one who is at all aware of having grieved or offended another, should without delay seek the one aggrieved, and by such explanations, confessions, and reparations, as may be demanded, remove the cause of grief.

NOTE 9.—If any member should attempt to bring before the church, or in any other way make public, any matter of private grief or offence, until he has fully pursued the above course, as prescribed in the Gospel, he becomes an offender himself, and subject to discipline.

NOTE 10.—If members become involved in personal difficulties, and make no effort to settle or remove them, or if they take any other course than the scriptural one set forth by the Saviour, they become themselves offenders against the church, and are subject to its discipline.

NOTE 11.—Where personal difficulties are known to exist, which the parties themselves will not, or cannot, settle, the officers or other members should use their utmost endeavors to reconcile and remove them privately, and avoid, if possible, bringing them before the church.

NOTE 12.—But when all private efforts fail to reconcile and remove such difficulties, the case should be taken up by the church, and treated as a public offence. The continuance of such things is greatly injurious to the prosperity of the body.

NOTE 13.—There may be instances of private offences, where, though the offended individual may be willing to dismiss the case, yet the church thinking its character compromised, or its welfare injured in the act, may find it necessary to take it up, and pursue a course of discipline with the offender.

NOTE 14.—When any member refers any private difficulty to the church which he himself has failed to settle, he should then leave it entirely in their hands, and be satisfied with whatever disposition they make of it, neither complaining at the result, nor attempting to prosecute it further.

Note 15.—Nothing can properly be considered a reasonable cause of offence, or matter of discipline, but what is manifestly forbidden in the Scriptures. Members may see things in others which they personally dislike, but which cannot justly be considered as subject to ecclesiastical complaint or discipline. They are matters for Christian forbearance, to be endured, if they cannot be corrected in some other way.

Note 16.—Nothing can be considered a just and reasonable cause for the withdrawal of fellowship, and exclusion from the church, except it be clearly forbidden in, or contrary to, the Scriptures, and what would have prevented the reception of the individual into the church, had it existed at the time, and been persisted in. Even these do not ordinarily lead to disfellowship and exclusion, provided they be confessed, repented of, and forsaken.

II.—Public Offences.

A *public offence* is one, not against any particular individual, but against *the church as a body;* an injury to the cause of piety, a reproach to the Gospel, a scandal to the Christian name and profession.

Every difficulty or offence, when it claims the attention of the church as a body, and comes before it, for its action, is a public offence. All those difficulties which individuals cannot appropriately reach or undertake; or such as they might, but will not attempt to settle; or such as having attempted, they fail to reconcile or remove, come within this class.

A. THEIR CHARACTER.

The following constitute the more common causes of public offence:

1. *False Doctrine.*—Holding doctrines fundamentally false, and contrary to the faith of the church, and the word of God. "If any man preach any other gospel unto you than that ye have received, let him be accursed."[1] "If there come any unto you, and bring not this doctrine, receive him not into your house, neither bid him God-speed."[2]

2. *Disregard of Authority.*—When a member refuses to regard the authority, and submit to the requirements of the church. "But if he neglect to hear the church, let him be unto thee as a heathen man, and a publican."[3] "Now we exhort you, brethren, warn them that are unruly."[4]

3. *Contention and Strife.*—Where a member is factious, foments discords, stirs up strife, and becomes a leader of evil, disturbing or destroying the peace of the church. "I beseech you, brethren, mark them which cause divisions and

[1] Gal. i. 9. [2] 2 John 12. [3] Matt. xviii. 17. [4] 1 Thes. v. 14.

offences, contrary to the doctrine which ye have learned, and avoid them."[1]

4. *Immoral Conduct.*—Such acts and practices as are inconsistent with that rectitude and purity of life, which the Gospel inculcates and requires. "But now I have written unto you not to keep company, if any man that is called a brother be a fornicator, or covetous, or an idolater, or a railer, or a drunkard, or an extortioner; with such a one, no not to eat."[2]

5. *Disorderly Walk.*—Such a course of conduct, or habit of life, as is contrary to, and subversive of, the professed faith, and established order of the church, of which the person is a member. It does not necessarily imply immorality of conduct. "Withdraw yourself from every brother that walketh disorderly, and not after the tradition which he received of us."[3] "There are some which walk among you disorderly, working not at all, but are busybodies."[4]

6. *Covetous Spirit.*—Where a member will not contribute according to his evident ability for the support of the Gospel, and refuses to bear his proportion of the pecuniary burdens of the church, evincing a covetous disposition. "For this ye know, that—no covetous man, who is an

[1] Rom. xvi. 17. [2] 1 Cor. v. 11. [3] 2 Thes. iii. 6. [4] 2 Thes. iii. 11.

idolater, hath any inheritance in the kingdom of Christ."[1] "If any man that is called a brother be covetous, with such a one, no not to eat."[2]

7. *Arrogant Conduct.*—Where a member in a spirit of pride and arrogance, assumes authority which does not belong to him, and undertakes to domineer over the members and to rule the church. "I wrote unto the church: but Diotrephes, who loveth to have the preëminence among them, receiveth us not, wherefore if I come, I will remember his deeds."[3]

8. *Going to Law.*—The going to law with brethren "before unbelievers," and the prosecution of each other before civil tribunals, instead of settling their difficulties "before the saints." This was severely censured by the Apostle, and deserves to be made a cause of discipline in every church. "I speak to your shame: Brother goeth to law with brother, and that before the unbelievers. Now, there is utterly a fault among you, because ye go to law with one another. Why do ye not rather take wrong? Why do ye not rather be defrauded?"[4]

[1] Eph. v. 5. [2] 1 Cor. v. 11.
[3] 3 John 9. [4] 1 Cor. vi. 6.

B. THEIR TREATMENT.

In cases of public offence, a correct course of discipline would be as follows:

1. The first member who has knowledge of the offence should, the same as in private cases, seek the offender; and if possible reconcile or remove the difficulty. This should be done because each member suffers in the wrongs of the church; and because such a course of private labor in a Christian spirit is most effectual. And if there are many pursuing such a course with the offender at the same time, so much the more effectual will it be.

2. But if no one can or will pursue such a course of private labor, or if such a course be unsuccessful, then any member having knowledge of the case, should bring it before the church at its next meeting for business. Before doing this, however, it would be prudent to consult with the pastor, and judicious brethren. It should be kept out of the church so long as there is hope of adjusting it privately.

3. The church having knowledge of the case, should call the offender before them to answer to the charge, where he should hear the evidence against him, know the witness, and be allowed to answer for himself.

4. If the offender cannot or will not appear before the church, they should appoint one or more, to visit and labor with him, and report the result to the church. The committee thus appointed should go in the name of the church, and invested with its authority, plainly making known the business; but they should go in the same spirit, and with the same design as if in a private difficulty they sought to gain their brother.

5. If in any case of discipline, and at any stage, the accused brother *disproves* the charge, or, in any ordinary case, if he admits it, *confesses* the wrong, makes suitable acknowledgment, and *reparation* as far as possible, together with promise of amendment, this should be deemed sufficient and the case *dismissed.* The purity of the church is vindicated, its authority sustained, and an erring brother brought back to Christ, and to his people.

6. But if, after patient, deliberate, and prayerful labor, all efforts fail to reclaim the offender; then, however painful the necessity, the church must *withdraw from him its fellowship.*

NOTE 1.—Every member tried by the church, has a right to require and receive copies of all charges against him, the names of his accusers and of the witnesses, both of whom he shall have the privilege of meeting face to face, hearing their accusations and testimony, bringing witness on his side, and answering for himself before the church.

NOTE 2.—Every person tried by the church should be allowed every opportunity, both as to time, place and circumstance, to vindicate himself. The very justice of Christ's house should incline to mercy.

NOTE 3.—Every member, whether on trial or having been excluded, has a right to receive authentic copies of the records of all proceedings held by the church in his case.

NOTE 4.—It would not be proper for any member on trial before the church, to bring a person who is not a member to appear as his advocate and plead his cause.

NOTE 5.—In every case of exclusion, *the charges* against the member, and the *reasons* for his exclusion should be carefully and accurately written out, and *entered on the records* of the church.

NOTE 6.—It is customary also, to *notify* the individual *of his exclusion*, by sending him a copy of the records of the final action in his case.

NOTE 7.—The church ought not to *entertain a charge* against any member, unless the evidence be such as to make its truth highly probable, if not certain.

NOTE 8.—Offences may occur of such an aggravated character, as to require, when fully proven, that the church should *at once withdraw its fellowship* from the offender, without any other attempt to labor with him, and notwithstanding all confessions, penitence and promises.

NOTE 9.—If the church shall find that it has *dealt unjustly* with a member, or excluded him without sufficient cause, it should at once proceed, of its own accord, and without his request, by *concession* and a *restoration*, to repair by every possible means, the injury it has done him.

NOTE 10.—The church should *not forget* those excluded from its fellowship, but kindly seek to do them good, and to reclaim them to godliness.

NOTE 11.—So also, should the church, at any time, be willing to grant a *rehearing*, if requested by an excluded member, providing he gives assurance that he can establish his innocence, or satisfy them by his acknowledgments.

NOTE 12.—The church should *restore* to its fellowship, at his request, any excluded person, whenever his reparation and confession for the past are satisfactory, and his present walk according to godliness.

NOTE 13.—Pastors, deacons, and *all officers* must be subject to the same discipline, and administered in the same way, as other members of the church.[1]

NOTE 14.—In all things, not contrary to his conscience, the *member* should submit to the authority of the *church*. But in all questions of faith and conscience, he should do what he believes to be right, even though the church should condemn him for it.

NOTE 15.—While on the contrary, the *church* must not fail to exercise its legitimate and rightful authority, and discipline its members for what it regards as sufficient cause, even though such members consider the discipline unjust, and think themselves injured by it.

NOTE 16.—No one while on trial before the church, can properly accuse, or bring charges against another member. His own case must first be decided on its own merits. If his offence be proven or confessed, no accusations made against others can justify it, or should be allowed. But any statement can be made, or evidence produced, which may tend to prove the innocence, or palliate the offence of the accused, even though such statement should implicate others.

[1] See First Part, chap. vii. 7.

CHAPTER X.

ITS BUSINESS.

MUCH of the harmony and prosperity of a church depends on the correctness and punctuality with which its *business* is transacted. All its meetings for business should be orderly and dignified, conducted rather in the spirit of devout worship, than of secular transaction.

That wisdom which cometh from above should be earnestly invoked, and allowed to prevail over all human counsels. Trifling and contention should have no place on occasions so sacred, while each one should seek, not his own, but "the things that are Jesus Christ's."

NOTE 1.—The pastor, by virtue of his office, is moderator of all church meetings. But in his absence, or at his request, another member may be chosen to fill the place.

NOTE 2.—Each church will determine what number shall constitute a *quorum;* but no important business should be done without a full attendance of the members.

NOTE 3.—All meetings for business are announced from the pulpit one Sabbath, at least, before they are held.

I.—Order of Business.

1. The meeting should be opened with reading the Scriptures, singing, and prayer, the same as meetings for worship.

2. If there are persons to be received as members, this is first done. The *experience* of candidates for baptism is heard, and the *letters* of those desiring to unite from other churches are read.

Note 4.—In some churches, members are received at the covenant, or other meeting, instead of at the church meeting.

Note 5.—It is customary for the candidates to retire while the church considers, and votes on, the question of their reception. This is desirable.

Note 6.—It is customary in most churches for all persons, except the members of the church, to retire from the meeting while the business is being transacted, unless specially invited to remain. This would be proper in all.

3. Next comes the reading of the minutes of the last meeting. This is properly the first item of business, but is usually deferred, where there are candidates for membership, till after their reception. If any mistakes or omissions are found in the minutes, they are corrected, and then are approved, by a vote—or without a vote, no one objecting.

4. Letters of commendation and dismission

are granted to such as desire to unite with other churches.

5. The unfinished business of the last meeting is next taken up and disposed of. . . . .

6. The reports of all committees previously appointed are received in their order.

7. New business, of whatever kind, is next presented. Any member may call up, or propose any new business; but if it be of a very special, or important nature, he should first have consulted with the pastor, deacons, or other judicious brethren respecting it.

NOTE 7.—Although the church should do nothing which it would be afraid or ashamed to have the world know, yet every member should regard himself bound by the honor of a Christian, not to publish abroad, nor repeat to those who are without, the private affairs and business of the church.

NOTE 8.—The established order of business may, for convenience, be changed at any time by a vote—or without a vote, no one objecting.

II.—RULES OF ORDER.

1. *Motions.*

a. All business should be presented by a *motion*—and in writing, if so required—the motion to be *made* by one member and *seconded* by another.

b. A question is not to be discussed, until it is

moved, *seconded*, and distinctly *stated* by the moderator.

c. After a motion is fully before the meeting, the mover cannot *withdraw* it, except by unanimous consent.

d. A motion should contain but *one distinct proposition*, or question. If it contains more than one, it may be *divided* at the request of any member, and the questions acted on separately.

e. A motion before the meeting, must be *put to vote*, unless withdrawn, laid on the table, or postponed.

f. A motion *lost* should not be *recorded* on the minutes, except so ordered by the meeting at the time.

g. A motion *lost* should not be *renewed* at the same meeting, unless under circumstances of peculiar necessity.

h. While a motion is under debate, no other motion can be allowed, except a motion to *amend*, to *substitute*, to *commit*, to *postpone*, to *lay on the table*, for *the previous question*, or *to adjourn*.

i. These last named motions cannot be interrupted by any other motion, except *to amend*, which may be done by specifying some *time*, *place*, or *purpose*.

j. Nor can these motions be allowed to interrupt or supersede each other, only that a motion *to adjourn* is always in order, (except *while one has the floor*,) and consequently supersedes all other motions.

2. *Speaking.*

a. Any one speaking on a question should *rise* in his place, and *address the moderator.*

b. If *two* members arise to speak at the same time, preference is usually given to the one *farthest* from the moderator.

c. No one should be *interrupted* while speaking, except he be out of order, or to ask, or make explanations.

d. No *unkind*, or *disrespectful* language, should be indulged in by the speakers, or allowed by the moderator.

e. Any member using improper language, introducing improper subjects, or otherwise out of order, may be *called to order* by the moderator, or any member, and must either take his seat, or conform to the rules.

f. A speaker may allow others to ask questions, or make explanations; but if he *yield the floor* to another speaker, he cannot claim it again as his right.

3. *Amendments.*

a. Amendments may be made to motions, by *omitting*, *adding*, or *substituting*, words or sentences.

b. Amendments *to amendments* may be made, but are seldom necessary, and should be avoided.

c. The *amendment* should be discussed and voted on *first*, and then the original resolution, as amended.

d. No amendment should be made, which *essentially changes* the nature or design of the original resolution.

e. But a *substitute* may be offered for any motion or amendment under debate, which may or may not change the meaning of the motion.

4. *Committees.*

a. Committees are nominated by the moderator, at the request of the meeting, or by the meeting itself; and their nomination is then confirmed by a vote.

b. Any subject in debate, or matter of business, may be *referred to a committee*, with or without instructions; the committee to *report* the result of their investigations to the meeting, and then action to be taken on their report and recommendations.

c. The *report* of a committee is *accepted* by a vote, which simply acknowledges the service of the committee, and places their report before the meeting for its action. Afterwards, any distinct *proposition* or *recommendation* contained in the report, is separately acted on, and may be *adopted* or *rejected.*

d. Often, when the recommendations of the committee are of trifling moment, or likely to be generally acceptable, the report is *accepted* and *adopted* by a single vote.

e. A report may be *recommitted* to the committee, with or without instructions, for a further investigation of the subject, or to present it in some form more likely to meet the concurrence of the meeting.

f. The first one named in the appointment of a committee is by courtesy considered the *chairman;* but the committee have the right to appoint their own chairman.

5. *Voting.*

a. Voting is done *by raising the hand*, or by "*aye*" and "*no*," the former of which is preferable in most cases.

b. In cases of special importance, voting by *ballot* is resorted to.

c. Voting by *standing up* is also done, when

it is necessary to count the affirmative and negative votes.

d. The vote is called by the moderator, first the *affirmative*, then the *negative*, so deliberately as to give all an opportunity of voting; he then distinctly announces whether the motion is *carried* or *lost.*

e. If the vote be a close one, and the moderator's announcement be *doubted*, he calls the vote again, usually by *standing*, and counts each side.

f. Members *under discipline* should not attempt to vote, nor take any active part in the business of the meeting.

g. The moderator has the right to give the *casting vote*, where the meeting is equally divided; but this right should be seldom, if ever, used.

h. All the members *should vote* on the one side or the other, except those under discipline, or unless for reasons they be excused.

i. No motion, discussion, or other proceeding, can be admitted while a vote is being taken.

6. *Appeal.*

The moderator announces all votes, and decides all questions of order, in debate; but any member who is dissatisfied with his decision, may *appeal* to the *meeting*. A vote then is taken whether they will "*sustain the moderator*." The decision of the meeting is final.

7. *Lay on the Table.*

Immediate and decisive action, on any question, may be deferred by a vote to *lay* the resolution pending *on the table*. This disposes of the whole matter for the present, and ordinarily is, in effect, a final dismissal of it; though any one has a right, subsequently, to call it up again. Sometimes, however, a resolution is laid on the table for the present, or till a specified time, to allow of other business necessary to be done.

8. *Postponement.*

An *indefinite postponement* is considered equivalent to a final dismissal of the question. But a question may be *postponed* for a specified time or purpose, and then resumed.

9. *Previous Question.*

Debate may be cut short by a vote to *take the previous question*; which means that the previous, original, or principal question under discussion, be immediately voted on, regardless of amendments and secondary questions, and without further debate.

a. If the motion for the previous question be *carried*, then the main question must immediately be taken without debate.

b. If the motion for the previous question be *lost*, the debate proceeds as though no such motion had been made.

10. *Not Debatable.*

Motions for the *previous question*, for *indefinite postponement*, to *commit*, to *lay on the table*, and *to adjourn*, are not debatable. But when they are modified by some condition of *time*, *place*, or *purpose*, they become debatable, and subject to the rules of other motions. A meeting is, however, competent, by a vote, to allow debate on all motions.

11. *To Reconsider.*

A motion *to reconsider* a motion previously passed, must be made by one who voted *for* that motion when it was passed. If the meeting votes to *reconsider*, then the original motion is before them, as at first, and may be discussed, rescinded, or reaffirmed.

12. *Be Discussed.*

If when any question is introduced, a member

objects to its discussion, as foreign, profitless, or contentious, the moderator should immediately put the question, "*Shall this question be discussed?*" and if voted in the *negative*, the whole matter is dismissed.

13. *Order of the Day.*

The meeting may decide to take up some particular business, at a specified time. That business becomes the *order of the day*, for the time specified, and must be taken up when the hour arrives, while all pending business is postponed in consequence.

14. *Point of Order.*

Any member who supposes that a speaker is out of order, or that the discussion is proceeding improperly, may at any time *rise to a point of order*. He must distinctly state his question or objection, which the moderator will decide.

15. *Privileges.*

Questions relating to the *rights* and *privileges* of the meeting, and of its members, are of primary importance, and for the time take precedence of all other business, and supersede all other motions, except that of *adjournment.*

16. *Filling Blanks.*

Where different numbers are suggested for filling blanks, the *highest number*, *greatest distance*, and *longest time*, are usually voted on first.

17. *Rule Suspended.*

A rule of order may be *suspended* by a vote of the meeting, to allow of transacting business which could not otherwise be done.

18. *Adjournments.*

a. A simple motion *to adjourn* is always in order, except when one is speaking, takes precedence of all other motions, and is not debatable.

b. A body may adjourn to a specified time. But if no time is mentioned, then it is understood to be adjourned to the time of its next meeting; or if it have no other fixed time for meeting, then an adjournment without date, is equivalent to a dissolution.

c. If a meeting votes to adjourn at a specified hour, no vote is requisite when that hour arrives. The moderator simply announces that the meeting stands adjourned.

CHAPTER XI.

ITS MISSION.

THE *mission* of the Christian Church is, to give the knowledge of salvation to the world, and so far as possible, persuade men to become reconciled to God—to accept the Gospel, believe in Christ, and be saved. In order to accomplish this, the church must present itself in a suitable spiritual condition, by maintaining itself in the faith and discipline, in the order and ordinances of the Gospel. Indeed, for this cause Christ gave himself for the church, "that he might present it to himself, a glorious church, not having spot, or wrinkle, or any such thing; but that it should be holy and without blemish."[1]

To fulfill its mission, it must exert its influence, as a body, on society, but especially must bring the piety of its individual members in contact with unconverted men. By a prudent and skillful improvement of those opportunities which Providence offers, and in a wise and judicious

[1] Eph. v. 27.

use of those means which may be used for the purpose, it must bring men under the influence of the Gospel, that they may be saved.

Every member of the church should have a part in this mission, and labor to fulfill it. There is work for all, and work adapted to the condition, ability, and capacity of each. Old and young, great and small, male and female, have something to do, and can do it. The efficiency and usefulness of a church, depends on each member filling *his own* place, and doing *his own* work, so as neither to be without work, nor attempt to do that of another. In nothing is the wisdom of the pastor and officers more apparent than in finding work for all, and giving something fit and adapted for each to do.

The common and ordinary means and methods of spiritual good to men deserve more regard than they receive.

I.—Gospel Ministrations.[1]

The preaching of the Gospel is the first and principal instrumentality for the salvation of the world. It is divinely instituted, and divinely sustained, sanctioned, and succeeded. The sacred promise is, " My word shall not return unto me

[1] See First Part, chap. vii.

void, but it shall accomplish that which I please, and it shall prosper in the thing whereto I sent it." [1]

1. The preaching of the Gospel in the *ordinary ministrations*, in houses of worship, as supported by churches. It is a part of the mission of the church to sustain the stated ministry of the word among them for the edification of the saints, and for the conversion of sinners.

2. They should also provide preaching with *unusual frequency* at times when Providence and the Spirit indicate special necessity for it, or special and unusual disposition on the part of the people to hear it, and to be benefited by it.

3. Preaching should be provided occasionally, or at stated periods, for such *destitute neighborhoods* and communities as may be within convenient distances of each church, and come appropriately within their sphere of influence, so that all the people may hear the word of God and the offers of salvation.

4. Each church should, to the utmost of its ability, assist in sending forth men to preach the Gospel to the *destitute everywhere*, beyond their immediate neighborhood and sphere of influence, at home and abroad, to the ends of the earth.

[1] Isaiah lv. 11.

NOTE 1.—Pastors of churches ought, as far as their strength and time will allow, to *cultivate* destitute fields adjacent to them. There is scarcely a church, in city or country, that has not some such out-station near it. These afford some of the most pleasant and profitable scenes of ministerial labor.

NOTE 2.—Some churches sustain a *colporter* or *missionary*, a part or the whole of the time, to labor in these destitute fields. This is an admirable method of missionary labor.

NOTE 3.—Some churches call into requisition, and encourage *lay-preaching*, for such purposes. In every church almost there are brethren who have more than ordinary gifts for exhorting and expounding the Scriptures, and ability to conduct religious meetings. But they do not consider themselves called to assume pastoral responsibilities, or technically to enter the ministry. It would be a great blessing to the churches and to the world if such gifts and abilities could be called into requisition for holding religious meetings in destitute communities, and bearing the Gospel to those who are without the ordinary means of grace.

II.—SABBATH SCHOOLS.

Next to the preaching of the Gospel, may perhaps be reckoned the *Sabbath-school*, as an instrumentality for religious good. The influence of the Sabbath-school is twofold. The *direct influence* on the pupils in moulding and forming their minds and characters as they expand; and the *indirect influence* through the children on their parents and households, and on their associates. The religious instruction and training of children, both in the household, and the church, is too little understood and appreciated. The character, and influence for good or evil, in subsequent life depends chiefly on the moral and religious training in childhood. Divine wisdom has provided for this, and enjoined that, "these words which I command thee this day shall be in thine heart: and thou shalt teach them diligently unto thy children, and shall talk of them when thou sittest in thine house, and when thou walkest in the way, and when thou liest down, and when thou risest up."[1]

1. The relation which the Sunday-school sustains to the church is somewhat indeterminate, and variously understood. There are *two* principal views and opinions entertained respecting it, somewhat different, though not conflicting.

First, That the school is created by, is dependent on, and under the absolute control of the church. In this case the church appoints its officers and teachers, yearly perhaps, the same as they would appoint a committee for any other specific work—either with or without instructions, with or without power to fill vacancies, as they may prefer. The church is responsible for its support, and under obligation to maintain a watchful guardianship over its welfare, and the man-

[1] Deut. vi. 6.

ner in which the work is performed. When the period of their office expires, they report to the church, which reappoints them, or fills their places with others.

Second, That the school is a benevolent association, like any other organized for a specific purpose, not created by, dependent on, nor under the authority of the church. In this case members from the same, or from different churches, organize themselves into a society, appoint their own officers, make their own laws, and govern themselves. The church sympathizes with them, allows them the use of its rooms in which to meet, and aids them at its discretion; but has no direct control over it, nor responsibility in it, any more than in the case of any other independent society.

NOTE 1.—Either of these plans and relations may be entirely proper, and in harmony with the genius of the Gospel, and with the government and discipline of the church. Whichever method is adopted should be clearly defined, and distinctly understood both by the church and the school. Of course in neither case can the church exercise any direct authority or discipline over any except its own members, to whom, in all cases, its jurisdiction is confined.

NOTE 2.—Where the school is sustained in their house of worship, and the officers and teachers belong to the same church, it seems most appropriate and desirable that it should be created by, responsible to, and under the authority of the church directly. The pastor and members ought to see that religious instruction is provided under their own inspection, for their own children, and know what kind of instructors and instructions they receive in this most important department of education. They should also be able to exercise control over any evils, errors or difficulties which may at any time arise in the school.

NOTE 3.—Where schools are remote from the church, the members connected with different congregations, and dependent on their own efforts and resources, the independent society plan would perhaps be the better method to adopt in their organization and government.

2. The *number of sessions* which a school should hold on the Sabbath must be determined by those who direct its services. In cities there are often *two*, in the country seldom but *one*. It is very doubtful whether more than one session, as a permanent regulation, is ever expedient, or on the whole, profitable.

3. The *character of the government* must be *paternal* and kind, where corporeal punishments and ordinary penalties are not resorted to, but the children are ruled by love.

4. *Singing* should constitute a large part of the exercises, being pleasant and agreeable to the children, while it is instructive, elevates the sentiments, and softens and subdues the ruder traits and rougher passions.

5. The *exercises* should be greatly *diversified*,

not long continued in any one direction, since the young soon weary of protracted application. For this reason the superintendent, the officers and teachers should possess great versatility of talent, and be inventive of expedients for keeping up the interest of the school.

6. Sunday-school *labor* is as great an advantage to the *officers* and *teachers* as to the pupils themselves. The effect of such labor on the intelligent practical piety of those who engage in it, is most admirable, and should encourage all the members of our churches to such labor.

7. The *libraries* of Sunday-schools deserve very special attention. These libraries, if judiciously selected, and properly used, constitute one of the chief means of doing good by the school. But the practice of admitting so largely works of *fiction*, though they be religious, must be condemned. The practice of having many books of general literature, for general reading, is of very doubtful propriety. The library should be composed almost wholly, if not exclusively, of sound and safe *religious* books, adapted in style to the minds of the young, and suitable for Sabbath reading. The judicious selection of books for a Sunday-school library is a more difficult task than for almost any other collection.

8. *Bible Classes* are a similar, not a separate department of religious instruction. These classes contain the older and more advanced portion of the youth, together with adults, associated for mutual study of the word of God. The formation of adult classes of this kind should be encouraged, on account of the great advantages which arise; and the young, when they suppose they have outgrown ordinary school classes, should if possible be retained in advanced Bible classes.

NOTE 4.—The practice of *committing large portions* of Scripture to memory is of doubtful advantage. It taxes the memory more than it benefits the heart. And frequently the nervous system is overtasked, and the health seriously impaired by the efforts of ambitious children in this direction. A better plan is to commit a limited number of verses, and see who will give the most correct account of their meaning.

NOTE 5.—The propriety of *giving premiums* is seriously doubted by many. If done at all, they should be awarded for the best conduct, and the best endeavors to learn, rather than for the greatest actual proficiency; that is, according to real *merit* as far as possible, rather than *apparent standing*.

NOTE 6.—Teachers should not be satisfied with the *mere routine* of the *question book*. But coming with a prayerful heart, seek to lead the pupils into the knowledge of their condition as sinners, and the love and grace of Christ as a Saviour.

NOTE 7.—*Parents* and *members* of the church not engaged in the school should often *visit it*, to stimulate the pupils, and cheer the teachers.

NOTE 8.—The *Pastor* should frequently, also, *visit* the school to show his interest in it, and keep a prudent watch-care over it. It gives him great influence with the young to do so.

III.—Religious Visitation.

Another means for accomplishing the church's mission, is that of systematically visiting, for religious purposes, all the families within a given district or circuit. It is presumed that pastors and ministers generally, will visit families for the purpose of affording them religious counsel, instruction and prayer. But few, however, consider the duty or appreciate the advantages arising from the performance of this work by private Christians. This ministry of Christian faith and love cannot well be over-valued, since "pure religion and undefiled before God and the Father is this, to visit the fatherless and widows in their affliction, and to keep himself unspotted from the world."[1]

1. Every church should undertake to secure the religious visitations of all families, without distinction, that are situated within certain prescribed limits. Let the whole field be divided into districts, and a certain number of families apportioned to each member, male and female, who can be induced to undertake the work. Let

[1] James i. 27.

these visitors report from time to time in the social meetings of the church the incidents they witness, and at the end of the year, make a full report of all the work done, with the results. Such reports will be deeply interesting.

2. Or, if the church, as a body, will not enter upon the work, let a few of the members agree among themselves to do so, and accomplish what they can. And should there be none to agree, let any single one who feels the importance of it, enter upon it alone and, as occasion offers, spread the results before the church. Such an example will stimulate others. The work will prove of immense value to those who do it, as well as to those for whom it is done.

NOTE 1.—These visits should be emphatically *religious*, and not merely social. All present should be inquired of whether they are Christians, and if they are desirous of, or attempting to become such. With such exhortations, instructions, and encouragements, as may be appropriate.

NOTE 2.—Where practicable, *reading the Scriptures* and *prayer* should accompany the visits. It may not always be possible, or at least consistent.

NOTE 3.—The distribution of tracts, or other religious reading, is of great advantage. A tract or book is left during one visit, to be replaced by another at the next. This system of religious visiting and distributing Bibles, and good books, is substantially the work which Tract Missionaries, Colporters and Bible Readers do with so much success.

NOTE 4.—The *sick*, *poor*, *afflicted*, and distressed should be the special objects of such visits, since they most need their advantages, and are in a condition most likely to receive benefit from them.

NOTE 5.—Cases of sickness, poverty, and want should be *reported to the church*, which ought promptly, according to its ability, to furnish temporal aid and relief, thus conferring blessings on both the bodies and the souls of men.

NOTE 6.—These visits should aim to secure the habitual *attendance* of all persons on *religious worship*, in some place, wherever they may prefer.

NOTE 7.—Another prominent object to be accomplished is to secure the *attendance of children* at Sunday-school. Any who can secure these objects may think themselves richly rewarded and blessed in doing good, though nothing else should be accomplished.

NOTE 8.—Such religious visits are most profitable if made *statedly*, once a month usually. In cases of sickness, destitution, or of religious seriousness, or where any special good promises to be secured, more frequent visits may be needed, lest some advantage or opportunity may be lost through neglect.

IV.—CHRISTIAN LITERATURE.

One of the most practicable and effective methods of bringing religious truth in contact with human minds, is in disseminating a sound and salutary Christian literature in society. Both for the edification of disciples, and to awaken the attention of the unconverted, religious reading is of very great importance. Every good book or periodical put into circulation is both a public and a personal blessing.

1. Every family should have a few carefully-chosen *books* of instructive and devotional religious reading. They are easily obtained, and at small cost. Many are not needed. A few read over and over again, until they thoroughly imbue the mind with their spirit, are better than many carelessly read, or not read at all. While so many families have masses of romances, novels, light and injurious reading, let every Christian household be furnished with a Christian literature.

2. *Church Libraries*, for the adult members of the church and congregation, are an excellent means of religious instruction, as Sunday-school libraries are for the young. The use of such books can be entirely free to the congregation, or used at a trifling fee, which may serve to replenish and increase the list.

3. *Religious Periodicals* are, if possible, still more important than books, not indeed in their intrinsic worth, but because they are so much more easily obtained, and so much more likely to be read. The expense of a religious newspaper, or magazine, is so small that the poorest can have one, if they desire to do so, and they are received by subscribers almost without trouble. While their value in a family is exceeding great, particularly to the younger members, it

is a matter of surprise that so few religious families take and read a religious periodical.

NOTE 1.—An easy and effective means of scattering religious truth in a community is to lend good books and periodicals from house to house. Few persons would neglect to read what was kindly loaned them, though they might not care to purchase, nor even read it, if it were their own.

NOTE 2.—If churches, or individual members who are able, would annually pay for several copies of religious periodicals to be given away, or sent regularly to persons and families not able themselves to pay for them, they would be doing a good work, and one worthy of Christian benevolence.

NOTE 3.—Every church member ought to feel under obligation so far as practicable to sustain, and give a wide circulation to denominational periodicals. These are maintained as the advocates of religious truth in general, but especially of those distinctive truths which are denominationally cherished and held as vitally important, and which are in this way more effectually defended and propagated than in any other.

NOTE 4.—The circulation of religious books and periodicals through the families of a neighborhood, as an instrumentality for doing good, is so simple and easily performed, that every Christian, even the weakest and feeblest, can take a part in such a mission, and greatly benefit others by the means

CHAPTER XII.

ITS CUSTOMS.

There are various *customs* held by the churches arising from the circumstances in which they are placed, and the discharge of general Christian duties. These customs are not matters of *faith*, nor enjoined by any scriptural authority, but merely the result of convenience, or expediency.

In each such case it is needful to know, that the custom is not *contrary* to Gospel precept and example, and that it conforms, in spirit at least, as nearly as possible to such precept and example.

I.--Councils.[1]

It often happens that churches having very difficult, or very important business to do, desire the advice and counsel of others. For this purpose, *councils* are often called. This may occur in cases of ordaining pastors, organizing new churches, and especially in the settlement of dif-

[1] See Second Part, chap. viii., 7.—First Part, chap. vii. 4, 5.

ficulties, which, on account of excited feeling or different opinions, may not easily be adjusted. Such is a very prudent and desirable course to be pursued; and yet, so far as practicable, churches should do their own work, in their own way, without the aid of councils, since it must be confessed that in ages past they have been the cause of great misfortunes to Christianity, corrupting its doctrines, perverting its practices, and destroying the independence of the churches.

The parties desiring a council, send letters to such churches as they wish to have represented, requesting them to send delegates—usually, the *pastor* and *two brethren*—to meet at a given time and place for a specified purpose. And these various delegates, when so convened, are an independent body, appoint their own officers, and can act, or refuse to act, as seems to them best; can give such advice as appears desirable in the case, and pursue their own course in the investigation of the matters before them.

In some parts of the country, particularly in the Southern States, it is customary, instead of a council, to call together the presbytery, that is, the ministers, only, in cases of ordinations, recognitions, and the like.

NOTE 1.—It should always be remembered that councils have

no ecclesiastical authority.[1] They can only *advise.* They differ from *committees of reference,* in being appointed by the churches, while committees are privately solicited, are without appointment, and act in their personal capacity only.

NOTE 2.—A council called by *one party* in dispute, without the consent or concurrence of the other, is termed an *ex-parte council;* if called by both parties, mutually, or in concert, it is termed a *mutual council.*

NOTE 3.—Parties calling a council usually appoint a committee to present the case to the council when convened, and to act and answer for them. But such committee is no part of the council, and cannot act with it.

NOTE 4.—Parties calling a council should refer the difficulties entirely to them, believing that the wisdom and piety of those whom they have called will secure a careful investigation, and a just decision of the case.

NOTE 5.—Though a council cannot compel parties to abide by their decision, yet they can refuse to act in the matter, unless the parties agree so to do.

NOTE 6.—It is desirable where difficulties need to be referred to a council, that all parties should mutually agree to refer, and unite in a call. But it is easy to see that parties might, often from the very conviction that they were in the wrong, refuse to do this. Such a refusal would make an *ex-parte* council necessary. Otherwise, the innocent would be compelled to bear a perpetual wrong.

NOTE 7.—Though no church is obliged to send delegates to sit in any council, yet a call from any respectable source should be courteously treated, and, if practicable, responded to, in the hope of doing good, allaying dissension, and promoting the peace and prosperity of Zion.

NOTE 8.—Councils should not be composed of partisans, nor those who evidently favor one side rather than the other. But

[1] See First Part, chap. vii. 4, 5.

persons should be called whose wisdom and piety, whose known rectitude and impartiality would be likely to secure just results, and give the churches and the community confidence in their decisions.

NOTE 9.—In the investigation and judgment of any case referred to them, a council should be careful to have all facts and evidences possible to be obtained, on both sides the question, and touching all matters in dispute, so as to render a just and impartial decision.

NOTE 10.—Parties calling a council should cheerfully receive its advice, and implicitly abide by its decision, unless such a course would, in their opinion, require them to violate their consciences, or go contrary to the word of God.

II.—ASSOCIATIONS.

A *State Convention* is composed of the pastors and delegates from the churches, in a single State, meeting once a year, at such time and place as they shall agree upon.

An *Association* is composed of the churches represented by the pastors and delegates appointed annually within a given district, usually smaller than a State, and of convenient access, meeting also once a year, as they may decide.

A *Ministers' Meeting* consists of the ministers located within a given and convenient district—meeting statedly, usually monthly, for mutual counsel and improvement, and to consider the welfare of the churches.

All such *Associations*, *Conventions*, *Ministers'*

Meetings and the like, are entirely voluntary. No church or individual is obliged to unite with them; and if so united, can leave them when they wish. But while they remain connected with them, they must submit to be governed by their regulations. Such Associations are for fraternal intercourse, mutual counsel, and individual improvement, and to further the general interests of religion within their bounds. They have no ecclesiastical authority. Their meetings should devote the largest possible amount of time to *devotion*, and but little to business and debate.

III.—Special Services.

The services attending the *dedication* of meeting-houses, *ordination* and *recognition* of pastors and of newly-organized churches, and others of like character, though prescribed by no scriptural authority, are nevertheless, as conventional usages, appropriate and profitable. Their order is arranged at the discretion of those who have charge of them.

IV.—Societies.

All *societies* for *Missions*, *Bible* and *Tract distribution*, and other purposes of Christian benevolence, are like Associations, *voluntary;* are of human, not of divine appointment; have no control over churches; and are not immediately controlled by them. Their design is to concentrate and give greater efficacy to the efforts of associated piety and benevolence, in the extension of Christianity.

Such societies should be as few in number, as simple in construction, and as immediately under the influence and direction of the churches as possible.

NOTE 1.—It may well be doubted whether the existence of missionary and other benevolent societies, *within a church*, acting in concert with larger external societies, is desirable, or to be encouraged. For though great good may at times be accomplished by these societies, and their aim be always good, yet there is great reason to fear, their tendency may be to divert attention *from* the *church*, as the divinely appointed organization, for doing this very work. They may also tend to relieve the church from a sense of its legitimate obligations by throwing the responsibility of benevolent action upon supplementary societies. And still more, they place the management and direction of such affairs in the hands of the *society* officers rather than in the hands of the *church* and of its officers.

NOTE 2.—It is a question of much interest, how far a Christian shall identify himself with those societies whose object is, the suppression of prevailing moral evils. It is certain that every Christian should encourage, and so far as he can consistently, aid every good enterprise. But it is equally certain, that no church member should form any connection with other societies or associations that will in the least interfere with the most faithful and perfect performance of all his duties in the church. The church is a society divinely instituted, for the accomplishment of all the objects which a pious charity may seek; and is as simple in its structure, and as efficient in its action as any other can possibly be; and its claims are first.

Note 3.—Yet it is but just to say that many moral and reformatory societies have accomplished a vast amount of good in the fields of human want, which without them would never have been accomplished. It must also be conceded that sometimes associations of Christian men may reach evils, suppress vices, and contribute to human welfare, where it would be very difficult if not impossible for the same individuals acting through the church, directly to accomplish the same objects. But still it must be urged, let not the greater good which the church is constantly performing on a broader scale, be hindered by any want of faithfulness or defect in personal duties on the part of its members by any such external benevolence.

Note 4.—As to the propriety of church members connecting themselves with *secret societies*, it may be said, that whether these societies are good or bad in themselves, all the advantages they offer may be obtained in other less objectionable ways; and since connection with them will be a grief to many, and is at best of very questionable propriety, the safer course by far, is to avoid them altogether.

CHAPTER XIII.

ITS DUTIES.

The church has duties peculiar to its organized condition, and which are entirely distinct and separate from those which attach personally to the individuals who compose it; duties which each member is to recognize and perform, because he is a member.

1. *Duties to itself.*

The church must care for and keep itself, as the "body of Christ," and "pillar of the truth," in a condition which shall answer its holy design. It must preserve its character pure and unspotted, putting away from it all iniquity and sin. It must preserve such order, and exercise such a discreet and faithful course of discipline, as shall maintain vigor, activity, and efficiency in the body. It must shun all alliances with wickedness, and let its unequivocal testimony be always boldly and distinctly given on the side of righteousness and truth, and against all wrong and evil.

2. *Duties to its Members.*

The church should have a kind and constant regard for the welfare of each of its members, however weak or low, considering them all as the members of one body, and seeking the best good of each, without partiality or distinction. It should throw around all, those safeguards to piety which may prevent their wandering; and when they wander, in the spirit of meekness, restore them. It should comfort the troubled, instruct the ignorant, strengthen the feeble, and encourage the fainting.

It should maintain, for their edification, the faithful ministration of the Gospel and its ordinances, that they may be built up, and established in the truth.

It should console the afflicted, minister to the sick, and supply *temporal*, as well as spiritual aid, to the poor and needy. It is a reproach to the church, when its poor members are compelled to receive supplies for the necessities of life from the charities of the world, ministered by stranger hands, or else pine in want, while their brethren have enough and to spare.

3. *Duties to the Ministry.*

So far as may be in its power, the church should labor to supply a gospel ministry for the destitute everywhere. But especially is it the duty of each church, to maintain that ministry in its own midst, by securing the labors of a pious, faithful, and competent man, as its pastor.

It is their duty to give that pastor their generous sympathy and confidence; to be respectfully affectionate, in all their intercourse with him most sedulously and sacredly to guard his reputation and influence. They should also give him a liberal and generous pecuniary support, which shall place him not only above absolute want, but also above the perpetual vexations and discouragements of anxiety and care concerning temporal things.

They should constantly sustain him by their prayers and holy living, sanctioning and seconding the Gospel he preaches; profiting themselves by his ministry, and commending its excellence to all men.

4. *Duties to the Cause of Christ.*

The church, while it labors according to its ability in its own sphere, for these objects, should also give its countenance and encouragement, its sympathies and prayers, to every true Christian disciple, and Christian church, of whatever denomination, in their efforts for the universal spread of the Redeemer's kingdom.

It should encourage and aid the work of missions, Bible distribution, Sabbath-schools, and the like, to the extent of its ability. It should also give its influence in favor of all consistent attempts to suppress evil of every kind, and in every possible way show itself the friend and patron of all virtue—the enemy and opposer of all sin.

5. *Duties to the World.*

The church owes many and important duties to the impenitent world. It is for the benefit of unregenerate men it is maintained, as the salt of the earth.

It should carefully and constantly furnish such opportunities and methods of religious instruction for children and the young, as shall, by the blessing of God, fortify them against the temptations of error and sin, imbue their minds with religious sentiments, and secure their salvation.

It should seek by the force of its godly examples and the influence of its pious spirit, to pervade and sanctify all departments of society. Civil laws and social institutions should feel the power of its salutary energy, and the best welfare of humanity be secured.

It should also, and especially, labor to give the Gospel to every creature, that whosoever believeth may be saved.

CHAPTER XIV.

ITS PRIVILEGES.

THE church, as the body of Christ, the light of the world, and the home of the redeemed on earth, affords peculiar privileges to all who enjoy its friendship or share its communion. Every Christian should live within the church, receiving its blessings and laboring for its welfare.

1. *Its Worship.*

True, its worship may be enjoyed by those who are not its members, but not to the same extent—not with that entire freedom, pleasure, and spiritual profit. How great a privilege this is those well know who have enjoyed it, and still ardently desire, but are deprived of it.

And of all the associations of men, the Christian Church alone furnishes thus the blessing of a pure and true spiritual worship for the people of God.

2. *Its Ordinances.*

For believers to be allowed the administration of Gospel ordinances—to be baptized into the Redeemer's name, and the likeness of his death—to take the sacred symbols of his dying love; these are privileges most sacred and important. They distinctly reveal the grace of God to sinners, and bring the penitent soul into closer communion with Christ.

3. *Its Fellowship.*

To enjoy association with the godly, share in their counsels and their friendship—having fellowship in their joys and sorrows, their sympathies and their prayers alike—encouraging each other's hearts, and confirming each other's faith, while as fellow-pilgrims they travel a toilsome path. These are blessings which the pure in heart will always prize, though the vicious and the worldly may neglect or despise them.

4. *Its Watch-care.*

Thus, also, is the favor great, that each can enjoy the watch-care of pious sympathy and of brotherly love from all the others. This kind care points out dangers to be avoided, and mercies to be obtained. It kindly takes by the hand, and gently leads, along life's rough places, the weak and the fainting; and in the spirit of the good shepherd, seeks out and restores the straying ones of the flock.

5. *Its Instruction.*

The church is the school in which the disciple is instructed and trained, from his spiritual infancy to his maturity and meetness, for the inheritance above. Chiefly by the ministration of the Gospel, but also by all the services and duties in which he engages—by all the discipline to which he is subjected—by all he suffers and all he enjoys—by all his own experiences of godliness, and by all his intercourse with others. These, sanctified and succeeded by the Holy Spirit, are gradually but constantly educating the disciple for more enlarged spheres of usefulness on earth, and for that higher state of service and of bliss for which he is preparing. They are constantly acting to dissipate his ignorance and his errors, and nourish his divine life, until he shall attain its full measure, and be complete in Christ.

Great are the privileges, rich the blessings, which Christ gives his people in and through his church.

CHAPTER XV.

ITS PIETY.

THE personal godliness of its individual members constitutes the piety of the Christian Church. Their practical conformity to the Gospel adorns the doctrines of the Saviour in all things. The cultivation and practice of that piety demands the serious and constant regard of every Christian.

1. *Prayer.*[1]

Prayer is one of the most important of *duties*, one of the most important of *privileges*. It is the Christian's "vital breath," his "native air."

(*a.*) *Secret Prayer.*—No one can long maintain the life of godliness, in his own soul, or honor his profession of love to Christ, or usefully perform the duties of a Christian, who is not in the daily habit of secret prayer. Every day should he retire to his closet, and free from all

[1] See Part First, chaps. v., ii.

outward and worldly interruption, hold communion with God.

On rising in the morning, and retiring at night, are specially appropriate, as occasions for prayer. Yet, besides this, it should be enjoyed as often as practicable. Indeed, a spirit of ceaseless prayer should be cherished, and the heart often be lifted heavenward in holy communion. Almost every case of backsliding begins in a neglect of secret prayer.

(*b.*) *Family Prayer.*—Every Christian parent should see that daily prayer be offered in the family. No day should pass, under the ordinary circumstances of life, but that the divine goodness be acknowledged at the household altar. Reading some portion of the Scriptures should accompany these family devotions; and singing also, where that is practicable. The whole service should be very short, lest it weary and be irksome, rather than pleasant. At such occasions, every member of the family should be present—especially should the children and domestics come under the sacred influence.

(*c.*) *Social Prayer.*—Every Christian should consider it a duty and a delight, to assist in sustaining those services of social worship, for prayer and exhortation, which the members of the church observe. It is a great help to piety, and indeed it is difficult for a church to preserve its spirituality and efficiency without it.

(*d.*) *Special Prayer.*—Every Christian should, also, make it a point to offer special prayer for the church, its pastor, the success and universal spread of the Gospel, the conversion of particular persons; in short, for all those objects which he is particularly desirous the grace of God shall accomplish.

2. *Reading the Scriptures.*

The Scriptures are able to make us wise unto salvation. By these alone is the knowledge of Christ Jesus our Lord. Therein is disclosed the character both of God and man; and the way of life is revealed to human wretchedness, in the word of God. "Search the Scriptures."

Their precepts enlighten the mind, their spirit sanctifies the heart; more to be desired are they than gold. An *ignorant* Christian is without excuse, with the Bible, the treasury of divine wisdom, in his hands.

While one should read the Scriptures with prayer, he should *pray* while reading the Scriptures, for the Holy Spirit to guide him to a correct and profitable understanding of them. Some single portion, treasured in the mind and made the theme of prayerful meditation, will prove of the greatest possible advantage to the Christian.

3. *The Communion.*[1]

A punctual and prayerful attendance on, and enjoyment of, the ordinance of the *Lord's Supper*, is far too little thought of, and too lightly esteemed, as an indication of personal piety, and also as a means of religious prosperity and growth in grace.

It is surprising that so many Christians can neglect that sacred symbolic rite. How can the disciple, who trusts in atoning blood for salvation, neglect the table where are spread the emblems of a Saviour's dying love? Shall we forget his example, and disregard what he bade his disciples to remember and do?

Some absent themselves from the communion from mere indifference, some because they are grieved with their brethren, and some because they do not think themselves worthy to be there. All these views are false, most unjust and ungenerous to Christ, and most injurious to themselves and to the church. The example is unhappy on others, and especially on the young members. No one ever found that a neglect of

[1] See Part First, chap. iii. 2.

the Lord's Supper has cured a cold heart, or reclaimed a backslidden life, or removed any grievance or difficulty from among brethren.

The humble, prayerful, and spiritually minded Christian, will esteem it one of his richest privileges, that he can come to the table of his divine Lord, and there remember and celebrate the love that saved him. It cheers his heart, it brightens his hope, and strengthens his faith; nor will he ever be absent from so sacred a place, when he can be there.

4. *Brotherly Love.*

The spirit and practice of *Christian harmony* and *union*, by which the disciples of Christ live together in the bonds of peace, loved and loving one another, bearing with each other's faults, and still being kind; this is one of the chief excellences of the Christian spirit and character.

This also constitutes one of the strongest arguments in favor of religion that can be urged on the impenitent and unbelieving. Hatred and variance, contention and strife, are not the spirit of Christ, and should have no place in the hearts or intercourse of his people.

5. *Benevolence.*

A generous *benevolence* the Gospel inculcates.

It was the spirit of Christ, and is the spirit of all his sincere followers. "Freely ye have received, freely give," not only the blessings of grace, but equally every blessing needed; all of which alike, are the gifts of our Heavenly Father's goodness.

To feed the hungry, clothe the naked, visit the sick, supply the wants of the destitute, is an honor to the Christian name. And to do this, not only to those who are of the household of faith, but even to the unthankful and the unkind, in imitation of the divine beneficence. It is a reproach to the Christian profession when its disciples shut up their bowels of compassion against the poor.

6. *Integrity.*

It might seem unnecessary to speak of the practice of *integrity* as a Christian virtue; yet, it should be constantly cultivated and observed.

The Christian should be a man of *perfect honesty* with both God and men; upright, just, and truthful in all his dealings, having a sacred regard for his word; pure in all his conduct, generous and honorable in all his dealings, and without reproach or blame before the world.

7. *Spirituality.*

The Christian should cherish that *spirituality of mind* which is the life of religion, and the opposite of worldlymindedness, selfishness, sensuality, and lust. To have the "conversation in heaven," and the affections set on things divine, this is the nature and delight of one who is born from above, and has a new heart and a right spirit renewed within him.

8. *Consistency.*

In nothing is Christian *consistency* more apparent and marked than in setting an example which will be *safe* for *others* to follow.

Let him shun every appearance of evil, by *avoiding* those habits, indulgences, and recreations which are of *evil tendency*, and would be dangerous, at least for others, to practice, lest some, unhappily following his footsteps, should fall and perish. The devout Christian will deny himself even lawful pleasures and pursuits, if there is danger that others may take occasion thereby to commit sin.

9. *Forgiveness.*

The spirit of *forgiveness* should be earnestly cherished as a vital element of piety. The

Christian should forgive the injuries and hostilities of the envious and the malicious; much more, the fancied or real wrongs of friends, even as he has been or hopes to be forgiven.

He should do good to them that hate him, and pray for those who despitefully use him. So Christ did; and so his disciples can best subdue their enemies and imitate their Redeemer. Much more should the offences which sometimes arise among brethren be freely and cheerfully forgiven.

10. *Self-Examination.*

But few Christian duties are more important, and perhaps few are more neglected than that of *self-examination.* It should be habitually and frequently performed, not so much because it is *pleasant* as because it is *profitable.* Because it reveals to the disciple his faults and his infirmities; shows both how weak and how unworthy he is, and thus enables him to guard against future temptations, and, most of all, drives him to the Mercy Seat, where alone his strength is to be found.

Without this exercise frequently resorted to, which indeed may be as painful as it is useful, the Christian can know but little of himself, and little of that grace which sustains him. But with it, every Christian virtue is cherished; he becomes humbly confident, and meekly bold, in the fight of faith, and adorns the doctrines of godliness and the profession he has made.

11. *Religious Fasting.*

There are different opinions entertained by the wise and the good, respecting *religious fasting* as a means of sanctification and growth in grace. It cannot, however, be doubted that the Scriptures give abundant countenance to the custom, and that many of the most conspicuous examples of personal piety mentioned there, either habitually or occasionally practised it—not to forget the example of our divine Redeemer himself.

In times of great trial or temptation, or at ordinary times, to gain higher degrees of religious joy, and greater spirituality of mind, or to secure greater spiritual blessings for others, many of the godly in all ages have been accustomed to retire as much as possible from the world, denying themselves ordinary food and the usual enjoyments and pleasures of life, and find the blessings they sought in devout humiliation, and protracted and earnest communion with God.

CHAPTER XVI.

ITS DOCTRINES.

All evangelical Christian churches profess to take the *Holy Scriptures* as their only and sufficient guide in matters of faith and doctrine. To believe what the Bible teaches in this respect —nothing more, nothing less—is to believe *right* —nothing more and nothing less.

It is contrary to the enlightened conscience and judgment of every Christian, for any church or individual to construct a religious creed, separate from and independent of the Bible, and require each member of a church to assent and subscribe to that, even though such a creed be professedly founded on, and in many things in accordance with, the Scriptures. If one believes what the Bible teaches, and as the Bible teaches, he believes enough.

But since different persons understand and interpret the Bible differently, and draw contradictory doctrines from the same Scriptures, it is perhaps desirable that each church and each individual should have carefully drawn out and written down, in concise and expressive language, what they understand the Scriptures to teach. These are sometimes called "*confessions of faith.*" They are the understood teachings of the Bible, expressed perhaps in other words for convenience, and are important as a standard of reference and information, briefly expressing and explaining what are believed to be the fundamental doctrines taught in the Scriptures, and are also a convenient method of ascertaining whether the faith of others agrees with, or is contrary to, their own.

The most of churches have a Confession of Faith printed and distributed among the members. These are not verbally the same in all churches, but substantially alike as to the doctrines they express. The following form, usually called the "New Hampshire Confession of Faith," is now extensively adopted by the churches North and East, while the "Philadelphia Confession of Faith," is very generally in use at the South. The latter is substantially the "London Confession of Faith," first published in the year 1689. It is much more full than the one given below, occupying too much space for insertion in this work, and is higher in its tone as to the doctrines of grace. They do not in any sense, however, contradict each other. Besides these, there are many others, adopted by single churches, or Associations, but with no very essential doctrinal differences.

These do, of course, set forth but a small part of what the Scriptures teach, and are simply designed to present a few of the leading and most prominent doctrines.

I.—The Scriptures.

We believe that the Holy Bible was written by men divinely inspired, and is a perfect treasure of heavenly instruction;[1] that it has God for its author, salvation for its end,[2] and truth without any mixture of error for its matter;[3] that it reveals the principles by which God will judge us;[4] and therefore is, and shall remain to the end of the world, the true centre of Christian union,[5] and the supreme standard by which all human conduct, creeds, and opinions should be tried.[6]

Places in the Bible where taught.

1 2 Tim. iii. 16, 17. All Scripture is given by inspiration of God, and is profitable for doctrine, for reproof, for correction, for instruction in righteousness; that the man of God may be perfect, thoroughly furnished unto all good works. Also, 2 Pet. i. 21. 2 Sam. xxiii. 2. Acts i. 16; iii. 21. John x. 35. Luke xvi. 29–31. Ps. cxix. 111. Rom. iii. 1, 2.

[2] 2 Tim. iii. 15. Able to make thee wise unto salvation. Also, 1 Pet. i. 10–12. Acts xi. 14. Rom. i. 16. Mark xvi. 16. John v. 38, 39.

[3] Proverbs xxx. 5, 6. Every word of God is pure. Add thou not unto his words, lest he reprove thee, and thou be found a liar. Also, John xvii. 17. Rev. xxii. 18, 19. Rom. iii. 4.

[4] Rom. ii. 12. As many as have sinned in the law, shall be judged by the law. John xii. 47, 48. If any man hear my words—the word that I have spoken, the same shall judge him in the last day. Also, 1 Cor. iv. 3, 4. Luke x. 10–16; xii. 47, 48.

[5] Phil. iii. 16. Let us walk by the same rule; let us mind the same thing. Also, Ephes. iv. 3–6. Phil. ii. 1, 2. 1 Cor. i. 10. 1 Pet. iv. 11.

[6] 1 John iv. 1. Beloved, believe not every spirit, but try the spirits whether they are of God. Isaiah viii. 20. To the law and to the testimony; if they speak not according to this word, it is because there is no light in them. 1 Thess. v. 21. Prove all things. 2 Cor. xiii. 5. Prove your own selves. Also, Acts xvii. 11. 1 John iv. 6. Jude 3d v. Ephes. vi. 17. Ps. cxix. 59, 60. Phil. i. 9–11.

II.—The True God.

We believe the Scriptures teach that there is one, and only one, living and true God, an infinite, intelligent Spirit, whose name is Jehovah, the Maker and Supreme Ruler of Heaven and Earth;[1] inexpressibly glorious in holiness,[2] and worthy of all possible honor, confidence and love;[3] that in the unity of the Godhead there are three persons, the Father, the Son, and the

Holy Ghost;[4] equal in every divine perfection, and executing distinct but harmonious offices in the great work of redemption.[6]

Places in the Bible where taught.

[1] John iv. 24. God is a Spirit. Ps. cxlvii. 5. His understanding is infinite. Ps. lxxxiii. 18. Thou whose name alone is JEHOVAH, art the Most High over all the earth. Heb. iii. 4. Rom. i. 20. Jer. x. 10.

[2] Ex. xv. 11. Who is like unto Thee—glorious in holiness? Isa. vi. 3. 1 Pet. i. 15, 16. Rev. iv. 6–8.

[3] Mark xii. 30. Thou shalt love the Lord thy God with all thy heart, and with all thy soul, and with all thy mind, and with all thy strength. Rev. iv. 11. Thou art worthy, O Lord, to receive glory, and honor, and power: for thou hast created all things, and for thy pleasure they are and were created. Matt. x. 37. Jer. ii. 12, 13.

[4] Matt. xxviii. 19. Go ye therefore and teach all nations, baptizing them in the name of the Father, and of the Son, and of the Holy Ghost. John xv. 26. When the comforter is come, whom I will send you from the Father, even the Spirit of Truth, which proceedeth from the Father, he shall testify of me. 1 Cor. xii. 4–6. 1 John v. 7.

[5] John x. 30. I and my Father are one. John v. 17; xiv. 23; xvii. 5, 10. Acts v. 3, 4. 1 Cor. ii. 10, 11. Phil. ii. 5, 6.

[6] Ephes. ii. 18. For through Him [the Son] we both have an access by one Spirit unto the Father. 2 Cor. xiii. 14. The grace of our Lord Jesus Christ, and the love of God, and the communion of the Holy Ghost, be with you all. Rev. i. 4, 5. Comp. ii. 7.

III.—The Fall of Man.

We believe the Scriptures teach that Man was

created in holiness, under the law of his Maker;[1] but by voluntary transgression fell from that holy and happy state;[2] in consequence of which all mankind are now sinners,[3] not by constraint but choice;[4] being by nature utterly void of that holiness required by the law of God, positively inclined to evil; and therefore under just condemnation to eternal ruin,[5] without defence or excuse.[6]

Places in the Bible where taught.

[1] Gen. i. 27. God created man in his own image. Gen. i. 31. And God saw every thing that he had made, and behold, it was very good. Eccles. vii. 29. Acts xvii. 26. Gen. ii. 16.

[2] Gen. iii. 6–24. And when the woman saw that the tree was good for food, and that it was pleasant to the eyes, and a tree to be desired to make one wise; she took of the fruit thereof, and did eat; and gave also unto her husband with her, and he did eat. Therefore the Lord God drove out the man; and he placed at the east of the garden of Eden, Cherubims, and a flaming sword which turned every way to keep the way of the tree of life. Rom. v. 12.

[3] Rom. v. 19. By one man's disobedience many were made sinners. John iii. 6. Ps. li. 5. Rom. v. 15–19; viii. 7.

[4] Isa. liii. 6. We have turned, every one to his own way. Gen. vi. 12. Rom. iii. 9–18.

[5] Eph. ii. 1–3. Among whom also we all had our conversation in times past in the lusts of our flesh, fulfilling the desires of the flesh and of the mind; and were by nature the children of wrath even as others. Rom. i. 18. For the wrath of God is revealed from heaven against all ungodliness and unrighteousness of men, who hold the truth in unrighteousness. Rom. i. 32; ii. 1–16. Gal. iii. 10. Matt. xx. 15.

[8] Ez. xviii. 19, 20. Yet say ye, Why? doth not the son bear the iniquity of the father? The soul that sinneth it shall die. The son shall not bear the iniquity of the father, neither shall the father bear the iniquity of the son; the righteousness of the righteous shall be upon him, and the wickedness of the wicked shall be upon him. Rom. i. 20. So that they are without excuse. Rom. iii. 19. That every mouth may be stopped and all the world may become guilty before God. Gal. iii. 22.

IV.—The Way of Salvation.

We believe the Scriptures teach that the salvation of sinners is wholly of grace;[1] through the mediatorial offices of the Son of God;[2] who by the appointment of the Father, freely took upon him our nature, yet without sin;[3] honored the divine law by his personal obedience,[4] and by his death made a full atonement for our sins;[5] that having risen from the dead, he is now enthroned in heaven;[6] and uniting in his wonderful person the tenderest sympathies with divine perfections, he is every way qualified to be a suitable, a compassionate, and an all-sufficient Saviour.[7]

Places in the Bible where taught.

[1] Eph. ii. 5. By grace ye are saved. Matt. xviii. 11. 1 John iv. 10. 1 Cor. iii. 5–7. Acts xv. 11.

[2] John iii. 16. For God so loved the world that he gave his only begotten Son, that whosoever believeth in him should not perish, but have everlasting life. John i. 1–14. Heb. iv. 14; xii. 24.

[3] Phil. ii. 6, 7. Who being in the form of God, thought it not robbery to be equal with God; but made himself of no reputation, and took upon him the form of a servant, and was made in the likeness of men. Heb. ii. 9; ii. 14. 2 Cor. v. 21.

[4] Isa. xlii. 21. The Lord is well pleased for his righteousness' sake: he will magnify the law and make it honorable. Phil. ii. 8. Gal. iv. 4. 5. Rom. iii. 21.

[5] Isa. liii. 4, 5. He was wounded for our transgressions, he was bruised for our iniquities; the chastisement of our peace was upon him; and with his stripes we are healed. Matt. xx. 28. Rom. iii. 21; iv. 25–26. 1 John iv. 10; ii. 2. 1 Cor. xv. 1–3. Heb. ix. 13–15.

[6] Heb. i. 8. Unto the Son he saith, Thy throne, O God, is for ever and ever. Heb. i. 3; viii. 1. Col. iii. 1–4.

[7] Heb. vii. 25. Wherefore he is able also to save them to the utmost that come unto God by him, seeing he ever liveth to make intercession for them. Col. ii. 9. For in him dwelleth all the fullness of the Godhead bodily. Heb. ii. 18. In that he himself hath suffered, being tempted, he is able to succor them that are tempted. Heb. vii. 26. Ps. lxxxix. 19. Ps. xlv.

V.—Justification.

We believe the Scriptures teach that the great Gospel blessing which Christ[1] secures to such as believe in him is justification;[2] that justification includes the pardon of sin,[3] and the promise of eternal life on principles of righteousness;[4] that it is bestowed, not in consideration of any works of righteousness which we have done, but solely through faith in the Redeemer's blood;[5] by virtue of which faith his perfect righteousness is freely imputed to us of God;[6] that it brings us into a state of most blessed peace and favor with God, and secures every other blessing needful for time and eternity.[7]

Places in the Bible where taught.

[1] John i. 16. Of his fullness have all we received. Eph. iii. 8.

[2] Acts xiii. 39. By him all that believe are justified from all things. Isa. iii. 11, 12. Rom. viii. 1.

[3] Rom. v. 9. Being justified by his blood, we shall be saved from wrath through him. Zech. xiii. 1. Matt. ix. 6. Acts x. 43.

[4] Rom. v. 17. They which receive the abundance of grace and of the gift of righteousness, shall reign in life by one, Jesus Christ. Titus iii. 5, 6. 1 Pet. iii. 7. 1 John ii. 25. Rom. v. 21.

[5] Rom. iv. 4, 5. Now to him that worketh is the reward not reckoned of grace, but of death. But to him that worketh not, but believeth on him that justifieth the ungodly, his faith is counted for righteousness. Rom. v. 21; vi. 23. Phil. iii. 7–9.

[6] Rom. v. 19. By the obedience of one shall many be made righteous. Rom. iii. 24-26; iv. 23-25. 1 John ii. 12.

[7] Rom. v. 1, 2. Being justified by faith, we have peace with God, through our Lord Jesus Christ; by whom also we have access by faith into this grace wherein we stand, and rejoice in hope of the glory of God. Rom. v. 3. We glory in tribulations also. Rom. v. 11. We also joy in God. 1 Cor. i. 30, 31. Mat. vi. 33. 1 Tim. iv. 8.

VI.—The Freeness of Salvation.

We believe the Scriptures teach that the blessings of salvation are made free to all by the Gospel;[1] that it is the immediate duty of all to accept them by a cordial, penitent and obedient faith;[2] and that nothing prevents the salvation of the greatest sinner on earth, but his own determined depravity and voluntary rejection of the Gospel;[3] which rejection involves him in an aggravated condemnation.[4]

Places in the Bible where taught.

[1] Isa. lv. 1. Ho, every one that thirsteth, come ye to the waters. Rev. xxii. 17. Whosoever will, let him take the water of life freely. Luke xiv. 17.

[2] Rom. xvi. 26. The Gospel, according to the commandment of the everlasting God, made known to all nations for the obedience of faith. Mark i. 15. Rom. i. 15–17.

[3] John v. 40. Ye will not come to me, that ye might have life. Matt. xxiii. 37. Rom. ix. 32. Prov. i. 24. Acts xiii. 46.

[4] John iii. 19. And this is the condemnation, that light is come into the world, and men loved darkness rather than light because their deeds were evil. Matt. xi. 20. Luke xix. 27. 2 Thess. i. 8.

VII.—Regeneration.

We believe the Scriptures teach that in order to be saved, sinners must be regenerated, or born again;[1] that regeneration consists in giving a holy disposition to the mind;[2] that it is effected in a manner above our comprehension by the power of the Holy Spirit, in connection with divine truth,[3] so as to secure our voluntary obedience to the Gospel;[4] and that its proper evidence appears in the holy fruits of repentance, and faith, and newness of life.[5]

Places in the Bible where taught.

[1] John iii. 3. Verily, verily, I say unto thee, except a man be born again, he cannot see the kingdom of God. John iii. 6, 7. 1 Cor. i. 14. Rev. viii. 7–9; Rev. xxi. 27.

[2] 2 Cor. v. 17. If any man be in Christ, he is a new creature. Ez. xxxvi. 26. Deut. xxx. 6. Rom. ii. 28, 29; v. 5. 1 John, iv. 7.

[3] John iii. 8. The wind bloweth where it listeth, and thou hearest the sound thereof, but canst not tell whence it cometh, and whither it goeth; so is every one that is born of the Spirit. John i. 13. Which were born, not of blood, nor of the will of the flesh, nor of the will of man, but of God. James i. 16–18. Of his own will begat he us with the word of truth. 1 Cor. i. 30. Phil. ii. 13.

[4] 1 Pet. i. 22–25. Ye have purified your souls by obeying the truth through the Spirit. 1 John v. 1. Whosoever believeth that Jesus is the Christ is born of God. Eph. iv. 20–24; Col. iii. 9–11.

[5] Eph. v. 9. The fruit of the Spirit is in all goodness and righteousness, and truth. Rom. viii. 9. Gal. v. 16–23. Eph. iii. 14–21. Matt. iii. 8–10; vii. 20. 1 John, v. 4, 18.

VIII.—Repentance and Faith.

We believe the Scriptures teach that repentance and faith are sacred duties, and also inseparable graces, wrought in our souls by the regenerating Spirit of God;[1] whereby being deeply convinced of our guilt, danger and helplessness, and of the way of salvation by Christ,[2] we turn to God with unfeigned contrition, confession, and supplication for mercy;[3] at the same time heartily receiving the Lord Jesus Christ as our prophet, priest, and king, and relying on him alone as the only and all-sufficient Saviour.[4]

Places in the Bible where taught.

[1] Mark i. 15. Repent ye, and believe the Gospel. Acts xi. 18. Then hath God also to the Gentiles granted repentance unto life. Ephes. ii. 8. By grace ye are saved, through faith; and that not of yourselves; it is the gift of God. 1 John v. 1. Whosoever believeth that Jesus is the Christ, is born of God.

[2] John xvi. 8. He will reprove the world of sin, and of righteousness, and of judgment. Acts ii. 37, 38. They were pricked in their heart, and said—Men and brethren, what shall we do? Then Peter said unto them, Repent, and be baptized every one of you in the name of Jesus Christ for the remission of your sins. Acts xvi. 30, 31.

[3] Luke xviii. 13. And the publican smote upon his breast, saying, God be merciful to me a sinner. Luke xv. 18-21 James iv. 7-10. 2 Cor. vii. 11. Rome x. 12, 13. Ps. li.

[4] Rom. x. 9-11. If thou shalt confess with thy mouth the Lord Jesus, and shalt believe in thy heart that God hath raised him from the dead, thou shalt be saved. Acts iii. 22, 23. Heb. iv. 14. Ps. ii. 6. Heb. i. 8; viii. 25. 2 Tim. i. 12.

IX.—God's Purpose of Grace.

We believe the Scriptures teach that election is the eternal purpose of God, according to which he graciously regenerates, sanctifies, and saves sinners;[1] that being perfectly consistent with the free agency of man, it comprehends all the means in connection with the end;[2] that it is a most glorious display of God's sovereign goodness, being infinitely free, wise, holy and unchangeable;[3] that it utterly excludes boasting, and promotes humility, love, prayer, praise, trust in God, and active imitation of his free mercy;[4] that it encourages the use of means in the highest degree;[5] that it may be ascertained by its effects in all who truly believe the Gospel;[6] that it is the foundation of Christian assurance;[7] and that to ascertain it with regard to ourselves demands and deserves the utmost diligence.[8]

Places in the Bible where taught.

[1] 2 Tim. i. 8, 9. Be not thou therefore ashamed of the testimony of our Lord, nor of me his prisoner; but be thou partaker of the afflictions of the Gospel, according to the power of God; who hath saved us and called us with a holy calling, not according to our works, but according to his own purpose and grace which was given us in Christ Jesus before the world began. Eph. i. 3–14. 1 Pet. i. 1, 2. Rom. xi. 5, 6. John xv. 16. 1 John iv. 19. Hos. xii. 9.

[2] 2 Thess. ii. 13, 14. But we are bound to give thanks always to God for you, brethren beloved of the Lord, because God hath from the beginning chosen you to salvation, through sanctification of the Spirit and belief of the truth; whereunto he called you by our Gospel, to the obtaining of the glory of our Lord Jesus Christ. Acts xiii. 48. John x. 16. Matt. xx. 16 Acts xv. 14.

[3] Ex. xxxiii. 18, 19. And Moses said, I beseech thee, show me thy glory. And he said, I will cause all my goodness to pass before thee, and I will proclaim the name of the Lord before thee, and will be gracious to whom I will be gracious, and will show mercy on whom I will show mercy. Matt. xx. 15. Is it not lawful for me to do what I will with my own? Is thine

eye evil, because I am good? Eph. i. 11. Rom. ix. 23, 24. Jer. xxxi. 3. Rom. xi. 28, 29. Jam. i. 17, 18. 2 Tim. i. 9. Rom. xi. 32-36.

[4] 1 Cor. iv. 7. For who maketh thee to differ from another? and what hast thou that thou didst not receive? Now if thou didst receive it, why dost thou glory as if thou hadst not received it? 1 Cor. i. 26-31. Rom. iii. 27; iv. 16. Col. iii. 12. 1 Cor. iii. 5-7; xv. 10. 1 Pet. v. 10. Acts i. 24. 1 Thess. ii. 13. 1 Pet. ii. 9. Luke xviii. 7. John xv. 16. Eph. i. 16. 1 Thess. ii. 12.

[5] 2 Tim. ii. 10. Therefore I endure all things for the elects' sake, that they also may obtain the salvation which is in Christ Jesus with eternal glory. 1 Cor. ix. 22. I am made all things to all men, that I might by all means save some. Rom. viii. 28-30. John vi. 37-40. 2 Pet. i. 10.

[6] 1 Thess. 4-10. Knowing, brethren beloved, your election of God; for our Gospel came unto you, not in word only, but in power, and in the Holy Ghost, and in much assurance, etc.

[7] Rom. viii. 28-30. Moreover, whom he did predestinate, them he also called, and whom he called them he also justified, and whom he justified them he also glorified. What shall we then say to these things? If God be for us, who can be against us? Isa. xlii. 16. Rom. xi. 29.

[8] 2 Pet. i. 10, 11. Wherefore the rather, brethren, give diligence to make your calling and election sure; for if ye do these things, ye shall never fall; for so an entrance shall be ministered unto you abundantly into the everlasting kingdom of our Lord and Saviour Jesus Christ. Phil. iii. 12. Heb. vi. 11.

X. Sanctification.

We believe the Scriptures teach that Sanctification is the process by which, according to the will of God, we are made partakers of his holiness;[1] that it is a progressive work;[2] that it is begun in regeneration;[3] and that it is carried on in the hearts of believers by the presence and power of the Holy Spirit, the Sealer and Comforter, in the continual use of the appointed means—especially the word of God, self-examination, self-denial, watchfulness, and prayer.[4]

Places in the Bible where Taught.

[1] 1 Thess. iv. 3. For this is the will of God, even your sanctification. 1. Thess. v. 23. And the very God of peace sanctify you wholly. 2 Cor. vii. 1; xiii. 9. Ephes. i. 4.

[2] Prov. iv. 18. The path of the just is as the shining light, which shineth more and more, unto the perfect day. 2 Cor. iii. 18. Heb. vi. 1. 2 Peter i. 5–8. Phil. 12–16.

[3] John ii. 29. If ye know that he [God] is righteous, ye know that every one that doeth righteousness is born of him. Rom. viii. 5. They that are after the flesh, do mind the things of the flesh; but they that are after the Spirit, the things of the Spirit. John iii. 6. Phil. i. 9–11. Ephes. i. 13, 14.

[4] Phil. ii. 12, 13. Work out your own salvation with fear and trembling, for it is God which worketh in you both to will and to do, of his good pleasure. Ephes. iv. 11, 12. 1 Peter ii. 2. 2 Peter iii. 18. 2 Cor. xiii. 5. Luke xi. 35; ix. 23. Matt. xxvi. 41. Ephes. vi.; 18. iv. 30.

XI.—Perseverance of Saints.

We believe the Scriptures teach that such only are real believers as endure unto the end;[1] that their persevering attachment to Christ is the grand mark which distinguishes them from superficial professors;[2] that a special Providence watches over their welfare;[3] and they are kept by the power of God through faith unto salvation.[4]

Places in the Bible where Taught.

[1] John viii. 31. Then said Jesus, If ye continue in my word, then are ye my disciples indeed. 1 John ii. 27, 28; iii. 9; v. 18.

[2] John ii. 19. They went out from us, but they were not of us; for if they had been of us, they would no doubt have continued with us; but they went out that it might be made manifest that they were not all of us. John xiii. 18. Matt. xiii. 20, 21. John vi. 66–69.

[3] Rom. viii. 28. And we know all things work together for good unto them that love God, to them who are the called according to his purpose. Matt. vi. 30–33. Jer. xxxii. 40. Ps. xci. 11, 12; cxxi. 3.

[4] Phil. i. 6. He who hath begun a good work in you will perform it until the day of Jesus Christ. Phil. ii. 12, 13. Jude xxiv. 25. Heb. i. 14; xiii. 5. 2 Kings vi. 16. 1 John iv. 4.

XII.—The Law and Gospel.

We believe the Scriptures teach that the Law of God is the eternal and unchangeable rule of his moral government;[1] that it is holy, just, and good;[2] and that the inability which the Scriptures ascribe to fallen men to fulfill its precepts, arises entirely from their love of sin;[3] to deliver them from which, and to restore them through a Mediator to unfeigned obedience to the holy

Law, is one great end of the Gospel, and of the Means of Grace connected with the establishment of the visible church.[4]

Places in the Bible where Taught.

[1] Rom. iii. 31. Do we make void the law through faith? God forbid. Yea, we establish the law. Matt. v. 17. Luke, xvi. 17. Rom. iii. 20; iv. 15.

[2] Rom. vii. 12. The law is holy, and the commandment holy, and just, and good. Rom. vii. 7, 14, 22. Gal. iii. 21. Psalm, cxix.

[3] Rom. viii. 7, 8. The carnal mind is enmity against God; for it is not subject to the law of God, neither indeed can be. So then they that are in the flesh cannot please God. Josh. xxiv. 19. Jer. xiii. 23. John vi. 44; v. 44.

[4] Rom. viii. 2, 4. For the law of the Spirit of Life in Christ Jesus hath made me free from the law of sin and death. For what the law could not do, in that it was weak through the flesh, God sending his own Son in the likeness of sinful flesh, and for sin, condemned sin in the flesh; that the righteousness of the law might be fulfilled in us, who walk not after the flesh, but after the Spirit. Rom. x. 4. 1 Tim. i. 5. Heb. viii. 10. Jude, xx. 21. Heb. xii. 14. Matt. xvi. 17, 18. 1 Cor. xii. 28.

XIII.—A Gospel Church.

We believe the Scriptures teach that a visible church of Christ is a congregation of baptized believers,[1] associated by covenant in the faith and fellowship of the Gospel;[2] observing the ordinances of Christ;[3] governed by his laws;[4] and exercising the gifts, rights, and privileges invested in them by His word;[5] that its only scriptural officers are Bishops or Pastors, and Deacons,[6] whose qualifications, claims and duties are defined in the Epistles to Timothy and Titus.

Places in the Bible where Taught.

[1] 1 Cor. i. 1–13. Paul... unto the church of God which is at Corinth... Is Christ divided? Was Paul crucified for you? Or were ye baptized in the name of Paul? Matt. xviii. 17. Acts v. 11; viii. 1; xi. 31. 1 Cor. iv. 17; xiv. 23. 3 John 9. 1 Tim. iii. 5.

[2] Acts ii. 41, 42. Then they that gladly received his word were baptized; and the same day there were added to them about three thousand souls. 2 Cor. viii. 5. They first gave their ownselves to the Lord, and unto us by the will of God. Acts, ii. 47. 1 Cor. v. 12, 13.

[3] 1 Cor. xi. 2. Now I praise you, brethren, that ye remember me in all things, and keep the ordinances as I delivered them unto you. 2 Thess. iii. 6. Rom. xvi. 17–20. 1 Cor. xi. 23. Matt. xviii. 15–20. 1 Cor. v. 5. 2 Cor. ii. 7. 1 Cor. iv. 17.

[4] Matt. xxviii. 20. Teaching them to observe all things whatsoever I have commanded you. John xiv. 15; xv. 1 John iv. 21. John xiv. 21. 1 Thess. iv. 2. 2 John 6. Gal. vi. 2. All the Epistles.

[5] Ephes. iv. 7. Unto every one of us is given grace according to the measure of the gift of Christ. 1 Cor. xiv. 12. Seek that ye may excel to the edifying of the church. Phil. i. 27. That I may hear of your affairs, that ye stand fast in one spirit, with one mind, striving together for the faith of the Gospel. 1 Cor. xii. xiv.

[6] Phil. i. 1. With the Bishops and Deacons. Acts xiv. 23; xv. 22. 1 Tim. iii. Titus i.

XIV. Baptism and the Lord's Supper.

We believe the Scriptures teach that Christian Baptism is the immersion in water of a believer,[1] into the name of the Father, and Son, and Holy Ghost;[2] to show forth in a solemn and beautiful emblem, our faith in the crucified, buried, and risen Saviour, with its effect, in our death to sin and resurrection to a new life;[3] that it is prerequisite to the privileges of a church relation; and to the Lord's Supper,[4] in which the members of the church, by the sacred use of bread and wine, are to commemorate together the dying love of Christ;[5] preceded always by solemn self-examination.[6]

Places in the Bible where Taught.

[1] Acts viii. 36–39. And the eunuch said, See, here is water; what doth hinder me to be baptized? And Philip said, If thou believest with all thy heart thou mayest. . . . And they went down into the water, both Philip and the eunuch, and he baptized him. Matt. iii. 5, 6. John iii. 22, 23; iv. 1, 2. Matt. xxviii. 19. Mark xvi. 16. Acts ii. 38; viii. 12; xvi. 32–34; xviii. 8.

[2] Matt. xviii. 19. Baptizing them in the name of the Father, and of the Son, and of the Holy Ghost. Acts x. 47, 48. Gal. iii. 27, 28.

[3] Rom. vi. 4. Therefore we are buried with him by baptism into death; that like as Christ was raised from the dead by the glory of the Father, even so we also, should walk in newness of life. Col. ii. 12. 1 Peter iii. 20, 21. Acts xxii. 16.

[4] Acts, ii. 41, 42. Then they that gladly received his word

were baptized, and there were added to them, the same day, about three thousand souls. And they continued steadfastly in the apostles' doctrine and fellowship, and in breaking of bread, and in prayers. Matt. xxviii. 19, 20. Acts and Epistles.

[5] 1 Cor. xi. 26. As often as ye eat this bread and drink this cup, ye do show the Lord's death till he come. Matt. xxvi. 26–29. Mark xiv. 22–25. Luke xxii. 14–20.

[6] 1 Cor. xi. 28. But let a man examine himself, and so let him eat of that bread and drink of that cup. 1 Cor. v. 1, 8; x. 3–32; xi. 17–32. John vi. 26–71.

XV.—The Christian Sabbath.

We believe the Scriptures teach that the first day of the week is the Lord's Day, or Christian Sabbath;[1] and is to be kept sacred to religious purposes,[2] by abstaining from all secular labor and sinful recreations,[3] by the devout observance of all the means of grace, both private[4] and public;[5] and by preparation for that rest that remaineth for the people of God.[6]

Places in the Bible where Taught.

[1] Acts xx. 7. On the first day of the week, when the disciples came together to break bread, Paul preached to them. Gen. ii. 3. Col. ii. 16, 17. Mark ii. 27. John xx. 19. 1 Cor. xvi. 1, 2.

[2] Ex. xx. 8. Remember the Sabbath Day, to keep it holy. Rev. i. 10. I was in the Spirit on the Lord's Day. Ps. cxviii. 24. This is the day which the Lord hath made; we will rejoice and be glad in it.

[3] Isa. lviii. 13, 14. If thou turn away thy foot from the Sab-

bath, from doing thy pleasure on my holy day; and call the Sabbath a delight, the holy of the Lord honorable; and shalt honor him, not doing thine own ways, nor finding thine own pleasure, nor speaking thine own words; then shall thou delight thyself in the Lord, and I will cause thee to ride upon the high places of the earth, and feed thee with the heritage of Jacob. Isa. lvi. 2–8.

[4] Ps. cxviii. 15. The voice of rejoicing and salvation is in the tabernacles of the righteous.

[5] Heb. x. 24, 25. Not forsaking the assembling of yourselves together, as the manner of some is. Acts xi. 26. A whole year they assembled themselves with the church, and taught much people. Acts xiii. 44. The next Sabbath Day came almost the whole city together to hear the word of God. Lev. xix. 30. Ex. xlvi. 3. Luke iv. 16. Acts, xvii. 2, 3. Ps. xxvi. 8; lxxxvii. 3.

[6] Heb. iv. 3–11. Let us labor therefore to enter into that rest.

XVI.—Civil Government.

We believe the Scriptures teach that civil government is of divine appointment, for the interest and good order of human society;[1] and that magistrates are to be prayed for, conscientiously honored and obeyed;[2] except only in things opposed to the will of our Lord Jesus Christ,[3] who is the only Lord of the conscience, and the Prince of the kings of the earth.

Places in the Bible where Taught

[1] Rom. xiii. 1–7. The powers that be are ordained of God. For rulers are not a terror to good works, but to the evil. Deut. xvi. 18. 2 Sam. xxiii. 3. Ex. xviii. 23. Jer. xxx. 21.

[2] Matt. xxii. 21. Render therefore unto Cæsar the things that are Cæsar's, and unto God the things that are God's. Titus iii. 1. 1 Pet. ii. 13. 1 Tim. ii. 1-8.

[3] Acts v. 29. We ought to obey God rather than man.—Matt. x. 28 Fear not them which kill the body, but are not able to kill the soul. Dan. iii. 15-18; vi. 7-10. Acts iv. 18-20.

[4] Matt. xxiii. 10. Ye have one Master, even Christ. Rom. xiv. 4. Who art thou that judgest another man's servant? Rev. xix. 14. And he hath on his vesture and on his thigh a name written, KING OF KINGS AND LORD OF LORDS. Ps. lxxii. 11. Ps. ii. Rom. xiv. 9-13.

XVII.—RIGHTEOUS AND WICKED.

We believe the Scriptures teach that there is a radical and essential difference betwen the righteous and the wicked;[1] that such only as through faith are justified in the name of the Lord Jesus, and sanctified by the Spirit of our God, are truly righteous in his esteem;[2] while all such as continue in impenitence and unbelief are in his sight wicked, and under the curse;[3] and this distinction holds among men both in and after death.[4]

Places in the Bible where Taught.

[1] Mal. iii. 18. Ye shall discern between the righteous and the wicked; between him that serveth God and him that serveth him not. Prov. xii. 26. Isa. v. 20. Gen. xviii. 23. Jer. xv. 19. Acts x. 34, 35. Rom. vi. 16.

[2] Rom. i. 17. The just shall live by faith. Rom. vii. 6. We are delivered from the law, that being dead wherein we were

held, that we should serve in newness of spirit, and not in the oldness of the letter. 1 John ii. 29. If ye know that he is righteous, ye know that every one that doeth righteousness is born of him. 1 John iii. 7. Rom. vi. 18, 22. 1 Cor. xi. 32. Prov. xi. 31. 1 Pet. iv. 17,18.

[3] 1 John v. 19. And we know that we are of God, and the whole world lieth in wickedness. Gal. iii. 10. As many as are of the works of the law, are under the curse. John iii. 36. Isa. lvii. 21. Ps. x. 4. Isa. lv. 6, 7.

[4] Prov. xiv. 32. The wicked is driven away in his wickedness, but the righteous hath hope in his death. See, also, the example of the rich man and Lazarus. Luke xvi. 25. Thou in thy lifetime receivedst thy good things, and likewise Lazarus evil things; but now he is comforted, and thou art tormented. John viii. 21-24. Prov. x. 24. Luke xii. 4, 5; xi. 23-26. John xii. 25, 26. Eccl. iii. 17. Matt. vii. 13, 14.

XVIII.—The World to Come.

We believe the Scriptures teach that the end of the world is approaching;[1] that at the Last Day, Christ will descend from heaven,[2] and raise the dead from the grave for final retribution;[3] that a solemn separation will then take place;[4] that the wicked will be adjudged to endless punishment, and the righteous to endless joy;[5] and that this judgment will fix forever the final state of men in heaven or hell, on principles of righteousness.[6]

Places in the Bible where taught.

[1] 1 Pet. iv. 7. But the end of all things is at hand; be ye therefore sober, and watch unto prayer. 1 Cor. vii. 29-31.

Heb. i. 10–12. Matt. xxiv. 35. 1 John ii. 17. Matt. xxviii. 20; xiii. 39, 40. 2 Pet. iii. 3–13.

[2] Acts i. 11. This same Jesus which is taken up from you into heaven, shall so come in like manner as ye have seen him go into heaven. Rev. i. 7. Heb. ix. 28. Acts iii. 21. 1 Thess. iv. 13–18; v. 1–11.

[3] Acts xxiv. 15. There shall be a resurrection of the dead, both of the just and unjust. 1 Cor. xv. 12–59. Luke xiv. 14. Dan. xii. 2. John v. 28, 29; vi. 40; xi. 25, 26. 2 Tim. i. 10. Acts x. 42.

[4] Matt. xiii. 49. The angels shall come forth, and sever the wicked from among the just. Matt. xiii. 37–43; xxiv. 30, 31; xxv. 31–33.

[5] Matt. xxv. 35–41. And these shall go away into everlasting punishment, but the righteous into life eternal. Rev. xxii. 11. He that is unjust let him be unjust still; and he which is filthy, let him be filthy still; and he that is righteous, let him be righteous still; and he that is holy, let him be holy still. 1 Cor. vi. 9, 10. Mark ix. 43–48. 2 Pet. ii. 9. Jude 7. Phi. iii. 19. Rom. vi. 22. 2 Cor. v. 10, 11. John iv. 36. 2 Cor. iv. 18.

[6] Rom. iii. 5, 6. Is God unrighteous, who taketh vengeance? (I speak as a man.) God forbid; for how then shall God judge the world? 2 Thess. i. 6–12. Seeing it is a righteous thing with God to recompense tribulation to them who trouble you, and to you who are troubled, rest with us—when he shall come to be glorified in his saints, and to be admired in all them that believe. Heb. vi. 1, 2. 1 Cor. iv. 5. Acts xvii. 31. Rom. ii. 2–16. Rev. xx. 11, 12. 1 John ii. 28; iv. 17.

SEEING THEN THAT ALL THESE THINGS SHALL BE DISSOLVED, WHAT MANNER OF PERSONS OUGHT YE TO BE IN ALL HOLY CONVERSATION AND GODLINESS, LOOKING FOR AND HASTING UNTO THE COMING OF THE DAY OF GOD? 2 Peter iii. 11, 12.

Covenant.

Having been, as we trust, brought by divine grace to embrace the Lord Jesus Christ, and to give ourselves wholly to him, we do now solemnly and joyfully covenant with each other, TO WALK TOGETHER IN HIM, WITH BROTHERLY LOVE, to his glory, as our common Lord. We do, therefore, in his strength, engage—

That, we will exercise a Christian care and watchfulness over each other, and faithfully warn, exhort, and admonish each other, as occasion may require:

That, we will not forsake the assembling of ourselves together, but will uphold the public worship of God, and the ordinances of his house:

That, we will not omit closet and family religion at home, nor neglect the great duty of religiously training our children, and those under our care, for the service of Christ, and the enjoyment of heaven:

That, as we are the light of the world, and salt of the earth, we will seek divine aid, to enable us to deny ungodliness, and every worldly lust, and to walk circumspectly in the world, that we may win the souls of men:

That, we will cheerfully contribute of our property, according as God has prospered us, for the maintenance of a faithful and evangelical ministry among us, for the support of the poor, and to spread the Gospel over the earth:

That, we will, in all conditions, even till death, strive to live to the glory of him, who hath called us out of darkness into his marvellous light.

"And may the God of peace, who brought again from the dead our Lord Jesus, that great Shepherd of the sheep, through the blood of the everlasting covenant, make us perfect in every good work, to do his will, working in us that which is well pleasing in his sight, through Jesus Christ; to whom be glory, forever and ever. AMEN."

END OF PART FIRST.

PART SECOND.

CHAPTER I.

DENOMINATIONAL PECULIARITIES.

How do Baptists differ from other Christian denominations? This question is often asked by persons imperfectly acquainted with denominational distinctions; especially young persons, desirous of uniting with Christian churches. To this question many Baptists themselves find it difficult to return a satisfactory answer, simply because they have given so little attention to that subject.

In nearly all matters of doctrine, all Evangelical Christian churches agree. The following are the essential points on which Baptists differ from others, and in all of which they appeal to the sacred Scriptures to justify their difference, and sustain their views. They profess to accept of nothing as a matter of religious faith and practice, unless it be taught in the word of God. Not what others believe or practice, but what the Bible teaches, is their creed.

1. As to *baptism*—they believe that *immersion*, or *dipping*, is the only way of administering this ordinance, as taught in the New Testament and practised by Christ and his Apostles, and the only way in which Christians can obey the command to be baptized.

Consequently the *mode* is essential to the ordinance; and nothing but *immersion* is baptism. Therefore persons *sprinkled*, or *poured upon*, are not baptized at all.

2. As to the *subjects* for *baptism*—they believe that the only suitable persons to receive this ordinance are those *who have exercised a saving faith in Christ*, and are regenerated by the Holy Spirit.

Consequently, unconscious *infants* ought not to be, and cannot scripturally be baptized, since they can neither exercise, nor profess that faith in Christ; and to baptize such is contrary to the teachings and practice of Christ and his apostles, and most hurtful and injurious to the spiritual welfare of the children so baptized.

3. As to the *subjects* for *church membership*—they believe that such persons only as are truly *regenerate*, and have been *scripturally baptized* on a profession of faith in Christ,

can properly become members of a Christian church.

Consequently, neither persons *sprinkled* instead of being baptized, nor *unconscious infants*, nor *unregenerate persons*, are suitable to become members of a church. To receive the unregenerate to its fellowship would destroy the distinction between the church and the world, and contradict the entire spirit and genius of the Gospel.

4. As to the *subjects* for *communion*—they believe that the Lord's Supper is to be partaken by *members of the church alone*, being such persons as are regenerated, and baptized on a profession of their faith in Christ, and are walking in the faith and fellowship of the Gospel.

Consequently, neither *unregenerate persons*, nor *unbaptized persons*, though regenerate, nor persons *walking disorderly* and contrary to the Gospel, even though baptized, can properly be invited to partake of this ordinance. Therefore Baptists do not invite *sprinkled* members of pedobaptist churches to their communion, because such persons are not scripturally *baptized*; nor do they invite *immersed* member of pedobaptist churches, because such persons are walking disorderly as the disciples of Christ, by holding membership in, and walking in fellowship with churches which receive sprinkling instead of baptism, thereby sanctioning and sustaining a perversion of Christ's ordinance, and a disobedience to his command. For the same reason they decline to commune in pedobaptist churches, as being contrary to good order.

5. As to *church government*—they believe that each separate and individual church is entirely *independent* of all other churches, persons, and bodies of men, either civil or ecclesiastical, and is to be governed by its own members alone, without the aid or interference of any other person or persons whatever.

Consequently, churches governed by popes, bishops, synods, presbyteries, conferences, or in any other way than by its own members directly and exclusively, are not constituted on the model of the primitive churches, nor governed according to the Gospel rule.

6. As to the scriptural *officers* in a church—they believe there are but *two*, viz., the PASTOR, called in the New Testament "bishop," or "overseer," "presbyter," or "elder," and DEACONS.

Consequently, those churches which admit more than *two* officers, or orders in the ministry, have departed from the Gospel rule, and the construction of the primitive churches.

CHAPTER II.

THE BAPTISMAL QUESTION.

WHAT is scriptural baptism? Or, how must baptism be administered, to correspond with the primitive practice and fulfill the command of Christ?

In answer to this question, Baptists declare that baptism, according to the New Testament, can be performed in no other way than by *immersing*, that is, by *dipping* the candidate in water, in, or into the name of the Father, Son, and Holy Spirit. But Episcopalians, Presbyterians, Methodists, Congregationalists, and some other sects of Christians, say that baptism may properly be administered in various ways; either by *dipping* the candidate in water, or by *sprinkling*, or *pouring* water upon the candidate; but because it is more convenient they practise *sprinkling* for baptism. If they are correct, then there are *three* ways instead of *one* by which this ordinance may be administered. But which are right, Baptists or Pedobaptists? To decide this question we must go to the New Testament. That alone is the source of authoritative teaching on this ubject. What is found there must not be perverted nor trifled with; and what is not there found, cannot be made binding on the conscience of the Christian.

But as the New Testament was written in the Greek language, which people generally do not understand, and the word *baptize* itself is a Greek word transferred into our language, in order to understand this question fully, it is desirable to obtain the opinions of pious and learned men, who have made the study of the Bible the business of their life, and are familiar with the language in which it was written.

I.—Evidence from Lexicons.

What is the true and proper meaning of the word *baptize*, or as it is in the Greek, *baptizo?* To ascertain this, let us ask men who are familiar with Greek words—men who have studied the history of Greek words—men who have made Greek dictionaries. What do they say!

Scapula says, the meaning of this word is "to *dip*, to *immerse*, as we dip anything for the purpose of dyeing it."

Alstedius says, "to baptize signifies only to *immerse*, not to wash except by consequence."

Stockius says, "properly it means to *dip*, or *immerse* in water."

Stephanus says, "to *plunge* under, or overwhelm in water."

Schleusner says, "properly it signifies I *dip*, I *immerse*, I immerse in water."

Donnegan says, "to *immerse* repeatedly into a liquid, to submerge, to sink thoroughly, to saturate."

Parkhurst says, "to *dip*, *immerse*, or plunge in water."

Liddell and Scott say, "to *dip*, repeatedly."

To the same effect is the testimony of Robertson, Pickering, Ewing, Greenfield, and others. In addition, the following commentators and scholars agree in the same opinion as to the meaning of the word *baptizo:* Witsius, Salmasius, Calvin, Beza, Vitringa, Limborch, Bishops Reynolds and Patrick, Drs. Bentley, Towerson, and Owen. Indeed, so completely are scholars agreed that baptize means to *dip*, that Prof. Moses Stuart, one of the best scholars America has produced, says, "*baptizo* means to *dip*, *plunge*, or *immerse* into any liquid." And he adds, "all lexicographers and critics, *of any note*, are agreed in this."

It must also be added, that not one of all these scholars was a Baptist; so that it was not from a desire to build up, or to please the Baptists, they expressed such opinions.

II.—Significant use of Baptizo.

The peculiar use of the word *baptizo*, in the New Testament, is interesting and significant, and must have been designed. Prof. Stuart, Dr. Carson, and the best critical scholars, have decided that this word means to *dip*, *immerse*, or *plunge*, and that it means *nothing else.* Now observe that this word *baptizo*, is the only word in the Greek language used in the New Testament to express or describe the ordinance of *baptism.* Why was this word used *exclusively*, rather than some other word, unless *baptism* was a specific act, which this word precisely expressed, and which no other word could precisely express?

Baptizo is used in the New Testament *eighty* times. In nearly seventy of these instances it is used to designate the ordinance of baptism. *Bapto* is used *three* times, and means to *dip*, but has other meanings in addition. This word, therefore, because it has other meanings, is never applied to baptism. *Rantizo* means to *sprinkle*, and is used *four* times, but never to express *baptism.* If, as some say, baptism may be performed by *sprinkling*, why was not this word used, which expressly means to *sprinkle?* *Louo* is used *six* times, and means to *wash*, but is in no instance applied to this ordinance. Why was that, if, as some say, the proper meaning of baptism is *washing?* *Keo* is found many times in its various, combinations, and means to *pour*. But it is never used to express or describe the ordinance of *baptism*. Why was not this word used, if, as some say, baptism may properly be performed by *pouring?*

Why, then, did our Saviour and his Apostles carefully select from all the words of the Greek language that *one* which alone means to *dip*, and nothing else, and use that particular word to express the ordinance of baptism, and *never in a single instance* use any other word for that purpose, while the Greek language affords a great variety of words definitely expressing the different uses and applications of water, any one of which might have been used to designate the ordinance of baptism, had it been so desired? Evidently because that by *baptism* they meant a *dipping*, just what that particular word did accurately and precisely express, and which no other could. If *sprinkling*, *pouring*, or *washing* had been intended, there were words at hand which would accurately have expressed those meanings. But such words were never used;

therefore it is certain that Christ intended no such acts in the ordinance of baptism.

III.—Circumstantial Evidence.

What do the circumstances attending the administration of baptism as described in the New Testament teach?

Christ, in his baptism *went down into the water*, and *came up out of the water;* certainly not for the purpose of having water sprinkled or poured on him. Philip and the Eunuch *went down into the water*, *both* of them. It is difficult to understand for what they both went down into the water unless for Philip to *immerse* the Eunuch.

The Apostle alludes to the mode of the ordinance, and speaks of "being *buried* with Christ in baptism." Rom. vi. 4; Col. ii. 12. His idea of baptism evidently was that of a *dipping*, a *submersion*, since he likened it to a burial. Archbishops Tillotson and Secker, Drs. Wall, Doddridge, and Whitby, Bishop Nicholson, Whitfield, Wesley, Clarke and Wells, in their comments on these passages declare, that this language alludes to the primitive mode of baptizing by *dipping* or *immersion*. It evidently can allude to nothing else.

IV.—Testimony of Commentators.

What do those learned and pious men who have written commentaries on the Scriptures say respecting the baptism of Christ, his Apostles and the early Christians? Do they suppose it to have been performed by *immersion*, or in some other way? Look at their testimony.

Witsius says: "It is certain that both John the Baptist and the disciples of Christ, ordinarily practised *immersion*, whose example was followed by the ancient church."

Samuel Clarke says: "In the primitive times, the manner of baptizing was by *immersion*, or dipping the whole body into the water."

Doddridge says: "It seems the part of candor to confess that here (Rom. vi. 4), is an allusion to the manner of baptizing by *immersion*."

Abp. Secker says: "Burying, as it were, the person baptized in the water, and raising him out of it again, without question, was anciently the more usual mode."

Abp. Tillotson says: "Anciently those who were baptized . . . . were *immersed* and *buried in the water*, to represent their death to sin."

Bp. Taylor says: "The custom of the ancient churches was not *sprinkling*, but *immersion*."

Vossius says: "That John the Baptist *immersed* whom he baptized, there is no doubt."

Grotius says: "That baptism used to be performed by *immersion*, and not by *pouring* appears both from the proper *signification of the word*, and the *places* chosen for the administration of the rite."

Cave says: "The party to be baptized was *wholly immerged*, or put under water."

Mede says: "There was no such thing as *sprinkling* used in baptism in the Apostles' days, nor for many ages after them."

Calvin says: "The very word *baptize* signifies to immerse; and it is certain that immersion was the practice of the ancient church."

Wesley says: "Buried with him—alluding to the ancient manner of baptizing by *immersion*."

To the same effect is the testimony of Archbishop Usher, Bps. Pearce, Nicholson and Burnett; Drs. Towerson and Hammond, Bossuet, Venema; Bps. Fell and Stillingfleet, Whitefield, Baxter, Locke; Drs. Whitby and Wall, and many others, eminent for piety and learning, and none of whom were Baptists.

V.—Evidence from History.

What do those scholars and learned men who have written histories of the churches in the times of the Apostles and early Christians, say of their practice as to baptism?

Mosheim, Gieseler, Du Pin, Waddington, and Neander, are best known as Church historians. They all agree that for about *two hundred and fifty years* after Christ nothing but *dipping* was practised for baptism; and that for *thirteen hundred years* it was generally practised by all Christian nations, even after *sprinkling* was used in cases of sick or feeble persons.

Works ascribed to Barnabas, the companion of Paul, and Hermas, mentioned by Paul, and which works must have been very early written; Justin Martyr, about A.D. 140; Tertullian, A.D. 204; Nazianzen, A.D. 360. Basil, A.D. 360. Ambrose, A.D. 374; Cyril, A.D. 374; Chrysostom, A.D. 398; all speak of baptism as a going down into the water, and being dipped, or washed in the water.

Dr. Wall, vicar of Shoreham, England, wrote a learned history of Infant Baptism, which so much pleased the clergy of the English Church, that when assembled in full convocation they gave him a vote of thanks for his able work. He says *dipping* was the primitive mode of baptism, and declares this to be so plain that, "One cannot but pity the weak endeavors of such pedobaptists as would maintain the negative of it."

DR. WHITBY, an able divine of the Church of England, and author of a Commentary, says: "And this *immersion* being religiously observed by *all Christians* for *thirteen centuries*, and approved by our church."

BISHOP BOSSUET, one of the most learned and distinguished of the French clergy, and connected with the Catholic Church, says: "We are able to make it appear by the acts of councils, and by the ancient rituals, that for *thirteen hundred years*, baptism was thus administered [by dipping] throughout the whole church, as far as possible."

STACKHOUSE, author of the well known History of the Bible, says: "Several others have shown and proved that this *immersion* continued as much as possible to be used for *thirteen hundred years* after Christ."

BRENNER, a Roman Catholic writer, as quoted by Prof. Stuart, says: "Thirteen hundred years was baptism generally and ordinarily performed by the immersion of a man under water: and only on extraordinary occasion was sprinkling or affusion permitted. These latter methods of baptism were called in question and even prohibited."

BINGHAM'S Antiquities of the Christian Church is probably the most able work in English on questions connected with ancient Christian customs. It is quoted as standard authority by nearly all writers on these subjects. Rose, in his Biographical Dictionary, calls the author, "One of the most illustrious scholars produced by the English Church." Bingham, in this learned work, says: "And as this [dipping] was the *original*, *apostolical practice*, so it continued to be the *universal practice* of the church for many ages." He declares this "*immersion*, or *dipping* of the whole body under water," was to show the death, burial, and resurrection of Christ, and the candidate's death to sin and resurrection to a new life. And he adds, "there are a great many passages in the epistles of St. Paul which plainly refer to this custom." He declares that so strictly was immersion adhered to, as never to be departed from except in cases of sickness. To prove beyond doubt that *dipping* was the primitive mode of baptism, he quotes many ancient and learned authorities, such as the following: St. Cyril, St. Chrysostom, St. Ambrose, Fourth Council of Toledo, Epiphanius, Tertullian, Theodoret, Ordo Romanus, Gregory's Sacramentarium.

With these writers agree many others. It must still be observed that none of these were Baptists; which fact presents in a still clearer light the inevitable convictions of truth in the testimony they give.

VI.—Practice of the Greek Church.

It deserves to be noticed that the Greek Church, so called in distinction from the Roman Church, and which extends over Greece, Russia, Abyssinia, Egypt, Arabia, Palestine, and other African and Asiatic countries, has always practiced, and continues still to practise, *immersion* in baptism. True, that church is superstitious and corrupt, like the Romish, embracing many errors in its doctrines and customs. Baptism is also administered by a *trine* immersion, or a thrice dipping of the candidate. Yet the *mode* they have preserved as at first instituted. Even their children they dip at the tenderest age, and that too in cold water, even in the severe climate of Russia and Siberia.

Dr. Wall declares, "The Greek Church, in all its branches, does still use *immersion*, and so do all other Christians in the world except the Latins. All those nations of Christians that do now, or formerly did submit to the authority of the bishop of Rome, do ordinarily baptize their

9

infants by *pouring* or *sprinkling;* but *all other Christians in the world*, who never owned the Pope's usurped power, *do*, and *ever did*, DIP their infants in the ordinary use. All the Christians in Asia, all in Africa, and about one-third part of Europe, are of the last sort."

The *whole Christian world*, then, practised *dipping* in baptism for *thirteen hundred years* as their common custom; and the greater part of Christendom do still practise it; that is, according to WALL, all those countries that never were in allegiance to the Pope, including Asia, Africa, and about one-third of Europe; to which about one-quarter of the United States of America may be added. The Baptists, therefore, have on their side the Scriptures, reason, history, criticism, and the practice of the great mass of professing Christians, so far at least as the mode of baptism is concerned. With this they ought to be content, in the assurance that they are right.

VII.—THE EXISTENCE OF BAPTISTERIES.

The question of *baptisteries*, or places artificially prepared for the baptism of candidates, deserves a brief notice, as it serves to illustrate the primitive and long-continued manner of baptizing by immersion.

At first, as we know from the New Testament

history, converts were baptized in rivers, pools, and fountains, whenever these might be found convenient for the purpose. But afterwards, as Christianity extended, and converts multiplied, and especially in large cities, convenience if not necessity required the construction of pools or fountains, expressly for the administration of the ordinance.

These places at first were, doubtless, very simple—merely open cisterns. Afterwards a roof or dome over the pool was added, as a shelter for the congregation. And finally they came to be built, with great care and elegance. They were usually constructed in a circular or an octagonal form, with the baptistery proper, or pool, in the centre, and the sides either open, or surrounded by cloisters, dressing rooms, or rooms for other religious purposes.

These buildings were separate and distinct from the church, but near to it; and were thus used from the *third* to the *sixth* century. During the latter part of the *sixth* century, baptisteries began for greater convenience to be built in the porch or vestibule of the church, and still later within the body of the church itself. But it was not until near the middle of the *seventeenth* century, that these baptisteries for immersion, gave place to mere basins for sprinkling. This change was made in England by the authority of the Westminster Assembly of Divines.

Dr. Wall says respecting this: "As for *sprinkling*, properly so-called, it was, at 1645, just then beginning, and used by very few. This learned Assembly could not remember that fonts to baptize in had been always used by the primitive Christians, long before the beginning of Popery, and ever since churches were built. And that basins, except in cases of necessity, were never used by Papists, or any other Christians, whosoever, till by themselves."

Dr. Cave says: "These baptisteries were anciently very capacious, because the stated times of baptism returning but seldom, there were usually great multitudes to be baptized at the same time; and then the manner of baptizing by immersion or dipping under water, made it necessary to have a large font likewise."

Bingham says: "In the Apostolical age, and some time after, before churches and baptisteries were generally erected, they baptized in any place where they had convenience, as John baptized in Jordan, and Philip baptized the Eunuch in the wilderness, and Paul, the jailer in his own house."

Dr. Murdock says: "The baptisteries were

properly buildings adjacent to the churches, in which the catechumens were instructed, and where were a sort of cisterns, into which water was let at the time of baptism, and in which the candidates were baptized by *immersion*."

TERTULLIAN says: "Peter baptized his converts in the Tiber at Rome, as John had done in Jordan; and there was no difference whether a man was baptized in the sea, or in a lake, in a river, or a fountain."

These facts relating to baptisteries as places for the baptism of converts prove conclusively, even if there were no other evidences, that baptism was performed by the immersion of the candidates, since structures and fonts of the kind could not have been made for the administration of the ordinance, had it been performed by sprinkling, or pouring water upon the persons, instead of plunging them into water.

Several of these ancient baptisteries are still in existence, and others are well known in the records of Christian antiquities; as those of Florence, Venice, Pisa, Naples, Bologna, Ravenna, and the Lateran at Rome. This last is considered the most ancient now existing. That at Pisa was completed in 1160, and is of an octagonal form, being about 129 feet in diameter, and 179 feet high. That at Florence is about

90 feet in diameter, octagonal in shape, with a lofty dome. These dimensions, of course, apply to the building, and not to the pool of water. That of St. Sophia, at Constantinople, was so spacious, as on one occasion to accommodate a numerous council which held its session in the building. The term *baptistery* was, as is evident, applied indifferently both to the pool or font, and to the building which inclosed and covered it.

For information on this subject, consult Cave's Primitive Christianity, Bingham's Christian Antiquities, Encyclopedias, Edinburgh, Britannica, Brand's, Relig. Knowledge, Americana, and Robinson's Hist. Baptism.

VIII.—The Rise of Sprinkling.

But how came it that the practice of immersion as the *mode* of baptism was ever departed from? And when and how did *sprinkling* arise to take its place? That question is readily answered.

The first recorded instance of any deviation from the apostolic practice of *dipping* in baptism, is that of Novatian, which occurred about the middle of the third century, or A.D. 250. This case is recorded by Eusebius, in his Church History, and Dr. Wall, in his researches, could find no instance of *pouring* or *sprinkling* earlier than this.

Novatian being sick, and as was supposed about to die, greatly desired to be baptized, and as it was thought he could not be *immersed* on account of his sickness, water was *poured* profusely over him, as he lay on his bed, so as to resemble as much as possible a submersion. But this was regarded at the time as a *substitute*, and not a valid baptism; because, when sometime afterwards, he having recovered, it was proposed to make him bishop, this was objected by many that he had not been *properly baptized*.

From that time, however, *pouring* and *sprinkling* were occasionally resorted to in cases of sick or feeble persons, hence called *clinic* baptism, because administered to candidates on their beds. But *dipping* continued the common practice. In the Romish church pouring was tolerated in the *eighth* century, and in the *sixteenth* century was generally adopted as a matter of convenience. It was not claimed, however, that this was according to apostolic usages, but that the church had a right to change ordinances.

Dr. Wall says, France was "the first country in the world where baptism by *affusion* was used ordinarily to persons in health." Of England he says, "The offices and liturgies did all along enjoin *dipping*, without any mention of *pouring* or *sprinkling*." About 1550, sprinkling began to prevail, being adopted first in cases of "weak children," and "within the time of a half a century, from 1550 to 1600, prevailed to be the more general."

The history of sprinkling as given in the Edinburgh Encyclopedia, under the article "baptism," is as follows. The first law to sanction sprinkling as a mode of baptism, was made by Pope Stephen II., in 753. "It was not till the year 1311 that a council held at Ravenna declared *immersion* or *sprinkling* to be indifferent." Before that time sprinkling had been resorted only in cases of supposed necessity. "In this country (Scotland), however, sprinkling was never practised in ordinary cases, till after the Reformation; and in England, even in the reign of Edward VI., immersion was commonly observed." But during the persecutions which followed the death of Edward VI., and the accession of the Catholic Queen Mary, many of the Protestants, especially the Scotch, fled to Geneva, where, under the influence and teachings of the celebrated John Calvin, they imbibed a preference for sprinkling. "These Scottish exiles who had renounced the authority of the Pope, implicitly acknowledged the authority of

Calvin; and returning to their own country with John Knox at their head, in 1559, established sprinkling in Scotland. From Scotland this practice made its way into England in the reign of Elizabeth, but was *not authorized* by the established church."

In 1643, the Westminster Assembly of Divines debated the question in convocation, whether baptism should be administered by *dipping* or *sprinkling*, both modes prevailing, and it being thought desirable that the practice should be uniform. The question was decided by *one* majority in favor of *sprinkling*—*twenty-five* voting for it, and *twenty-four* for *immersion*. So near did the Church of England come to being immersionists. A year later, parliament sanctioned the decision of the Assembly, and enacted that *sprinkling* should be the legal mode of administering baptism.

IX.—Objections Answered.

Some Pedobaptists, with more zeal than either discretion or learning, have objected to *immersion* as the primitive mode of baptism, saying the Jordan had not sufficient depth of water for dipping candidates, and that Jerusalem had no conveniencies for the immersion of the thousands converted under the Apostles' preaching. Let such persons consider the following facts:

1. In 1848, Lieut. Lynch, in the United States service, was sent by our government in command of an expedition to explore the Jordan and the Dead Sea. He passed the entire length of the Jordan in boats, and made constant and accurate examination of all its features. These were recorded and published. He found the river varying in width from seventy-five to two hundred feet, and its depth from *three* to *twelve* feet. At Bethabara, where tradition has fixed the place of our Saviour's baptism, and where John baptized the multitudes, Lieut. Lynch gives the width as one hundred and twenty feet, and the greatest depth as *twelve feet.* To this place thousands of pilgrims continue to come every year, at a certain season, to *bathe* in the waters where they believe Christ was baptized. The expedition witnessed one of these occasions, and had their boats in readiness to prevent accidents, which were liable to occur while the multitudes were bathing. There is certainly no lack of water there.

2. In Jerusalem there were anciently several cisterns, or pools of large size, sufficient to accommodate hundreds of bathers at the same time. Outside, but near the city, were others of still

larger capacity. These were constructed partly to afford opportunity for the many ablutions required by the Mosaic law, and partly to supply the city with water. Some of them still contain water, and afford admirable convenience for the administration of baptism. Others are in a ruined state, but distinctly show their original construction and capacity. The most of them were in repair, and continued to be used, for hundreds of years after Christ, as history proves.

According to Dr. Robinson, who visited Jerusalem recently, and made accurate measurement of these pools, there are even now most abundant opportunities for baptizing. His statements are fully corroborated by Dr. Sampson, who has verified them by personal observation. The pool of *Bethesda* is 360 feet long, 130 feet wide, and 75 feet deep; and when it was full of water was a considerable pond, covering more than an acre of ground. The pool of *Siloam*, 53 feet long, 18 feet wide, and 19 feet deep, has now a depth of 2 or 3 feet, but can easily be increased to a much greater depth. The *Upper Pool*, 316 feet long, 218 feet wide, 18 feet deep, and covers an acre and a half of ground. The *Pool of Hezekiah*, 240 feet long, 144 wide, partly filled with water. The *Lower Pool of Gihon*, 592 feet long, 260 feet wide, 40 feet deep, and covers more than *three-and-a-half acres.* This pool is now dry, but as late as the time of the Crusaders was abundantly supplied with water, and free to the use of all. Several others are also found. These pools were all constructed with the sides gradually sloping, so as to make a descent into them perfectly convenient, to any desired depth. These statements are abundantly justified by Dr. Barclay, missionary at Jerusalem, and the most competent and reliable of all authorities on this subject, so far as the city of Jerusalem is concerned.

Such facts show how entirely gratuitous, and destitute of reason, are all objections to immersion as the primitive mode of baptism, on the ground of an insufficiency of water, either at the Jordan or in Jerusalem. And these investigations and measurements were not made by Baptists for the purpose of establishing a theory, but by Pedobaptists, for the purpose of scientific and antiquarian research. They do, however, most fully vindicate the truth.

CHAPTER III.

THE QUESTION OF INFANT BAPTISM.

BAPTISTS believe that no person should be baptized, except on a profession of faith in Christ. Since *infants* are incapable of exercising or professing that faith, they evidently are not proper subjects for baptism; and to baptize them would be both unauthorized and wrong. Pedobaptists, on the contrary, believe in and practise *infant baptism* as right and scriptural. Which are correct? Which act according to the teachings of the New Testament and the practice of the apostles?

Baptists assert the following facts:

1. That in the New Testament there is neither precept nor example to authorize or sanction the practice, nor even an allusion to the baptism of infants.

2. That Christ did not command it, and neither the Apostles nor early Christians practised it.

3. That it arose with, and was a part of, the early corruption of the Christian Church.

4. That it is presumptuous and censurable on

the part of parents, sponsors, and administrators, and productive of great evil to the child which receives it, and to the church which allows it.

I.—When did Infant Baptism arise?

The first mention of it in history is made by Tertullian, the beginning of the *third century;* and he opposes it, and speaks of it as a practice of neither long standing nor general observance. Bingham, before mentioned, believes it existed at an earlier period, which he is anxious to prove by vague inferences and obscure allusions. Yet this mention of it by Tertullian is the earliest he was able to find; though it is certain he would have found it, had there been any earlier reference to it accessible.

Bp. Burnett says, "There is no express precept or rule given in the New Testament for the baptism of infants."

Luther says, "It cannot be proved by the sacred Scripture that infant baptism was instituted by Christ, or begun by the first Christians after the Apostles."

Goodwin says, "Baptism supposes regeneration sure in itself first. Read all the Acts, still it is said, they *believed* and were baptized."

Limborch says, "There is no instance can be produced from which it may indisputably be inferred that any *child* was baptized by the Apostles."

BAXTER says, "I conclude that all examples of baptism in Scripture do mention only the administration of it to the *professors of saving faith:* and the precepts give us no other direction."

CURCELLEUS says, the baptism of *infants* in the *two first centuries* after Christ was altogether unknown; but in the *third* and *fourth* was allowed by *some few.* In the *fifth* and following ages it was generally received."

Dr. WALL, the ablest defender and most learned advocate of infant baptism, says, "Among all the persons that are recorded as baptized by the Apostles, there is no express mention of any infants."

NEANDER, perhaps the most learned and reliable of all church historians, says, "Baptism was administered at first only to *adults*, as men were accustomed to conceive of *baptism* and *faith* as strictly connected."

HIPPOLYTUS, bishop of Pontus, who wrote in the first half of the *third* century, says, "We in our days never defended the baptism of children, which in our day had only begun to be practised in some regions." "The baptism of infants we did not know." And Bunsen, his learned translator, declares that *infant baptism*, in the modern sense, was utterly unknown in the early church, to the middle of the third century.

Dr. HANNA says, "Scripture knows nothing of the baptism of infants."

Prof. JACOBI says, "Infant baptism was established neither by Christ nor the Apostles."

Similar concessions have been made by Erasmus, Calvin, Vives, Taylor, Mosheim, Gieseler, Coleman, Meyer, De Wett, Olshausen, Lange, Hodge, Stuart, Woods, and others, though at the same time justifying the practice on other grounds. They are agreed that Tertullian is the first writer who distinctly mentions the practice, and that it must have arisen about that time, A.D. 204. Had it been much earlier, it would have been mentioned by some earlier writer.

II.—FROM WHAT CAUSE DID IT ARISE?

The answer to this question is plain, and should be satisfactory. Soon after the ascension of our Saviour, various heresies arose and were mingled with the doctrines of the Gospel, and many superstitious rites corrupted the simple ordinances of Christianity. In this, all scholars and historians are agreed. Very early the notion began to prevail that the ordinances possessed a mysterious efficacy, a sanctifying power, and that to die without receiving Baptism and the Supper, was to endanger the salvation of the soul. Thus parents, very naturally being desirous of making certain the salvation of their children by every possible means, began to request baptism for them, thereby to insure their spiritual safety. This was at first, probably, done only in the cases of sick or dying children, but afterwards it became general. It was essentially the same idea as that which led to the practice of sprinkling for baptism—a false notion of the efficacy of the ordinance. No one who carefully reads the early history of Christianity can fail to see the correctness of this explanation.

CHAPTER IV.

THE COMMUNION QUESTION.

There exists, between Baptists and Pedobaptists, a difference of opinion respecting the question of Church Communion, as to who are properly qualified to partake of the Lord's Supper, and what are the scriptural qualifications. Both hold that baptism necessarily precedes the communion as a qualification for its privileges, and that *baptized believers* in Christ only, are to be invited to it. But what is Baptism? Pedobaptists assert that persons sprinkled, poured upon, or immersed, are properly baptized, and therefore invite such persons to the Lord's table. Baptists, however, declare that persons immersed *only* are baptized, and therefore invite none others to the Lord's table.

This practice of Pedobaptists is called *open*, or free communion, because it embraces the different denominations of evangelical Christians. The practice of Baptists is commonly called *close*, or restricted communion, because it restricts or confines the privileges of the Lord's Supper to immersed believers. These terms, however, are not very truthful or accurate, since *both* practise a restricted communion, and both adopt the same rule, and advocate the same principles, as to the terms of communion; while the real difference lies in their different views of what constitutes baptism.

But the question of Baptism is not the only question. Are there other qualifications prerequisite to the communion? And if so, what are they? And who is to decide whether these qualifications exist, whether these conditions have been complied with—the church or the communicant? These questions involve the vital elements of church structure, and of church order.

I.—Subjects of Communion.

Let us inquire who are entitled, and have a right to, the privileges of the Lord's Supper. May all persons, without distinction, who desire to do so, partake of it? If so, that would constitute, in fact, an open, or free communion—and in reality, that is the *only* open communion. Or, must this privilege be restricted to regenerate persons, believers in Christ? If so, then who is to be the judge of their faith, whether they are regenerate persons? Must the church to which they come decide this question, or may the individuals themselves decide it?

Still more, if the privilege is to be restricted to believers, and none but regenerate persons are to be admitted, then are *all* believers, all regenerate persons, to be so admitted without any further condition or qualification? Is regeneration the only test? Or must they also be first baptized, and be found walking in godliness of life? And who is to judge whether these conditions have been strictly complied with? Is the *church* to exercise this jurisdiction and right of judgment, or is it to be left wholly to the private convictions of the *individual*, to decide the question of his own fitness?

II.—Open Communionists.

The advocates of what is called *open communion*, are of three classes.

1. Those who hold that baptism is a necessary condition of, and prerequisite to the Lord's Supper, but assert that *pouring*, *sprinkling*, and *immersing*, are all, and equally, lawful and scriptural modes of baptism; and therefore persons baptized by either mode, and living correct Christian lives, are qualified subjects for the Lord's Supper. Of this class are Pedobaptists generally of the various denominations.

2. Those who agree that baptism is a prerequisite to the communion, and who believe that nothing but *immersion* is scriptural baptism, but who hold that the conscientious convictions of the individuals themselves rather than the judgment of the church, are to be taken as the rule of action. Consequently, if the individual believes himself to have been properly baptized, when he was sprinkled, and desires the communion, he should be admitted to the table on his own faith in the validity of his baptism, though the church does not believe he has been baptized at all. Of this class are immersed members of Pedobaptist churches, and the greater part of Open Communion Baptists.

3. Those who deny that baptism is a necessary condition of, or prerequisite to the communion, at all, and hold that there is no fixed order in the ordinances, by which Baptism must precede the Supper, but that the Supper may be lawfully received by those who have never been baptized in any way. Consequently, they would have the communion allowed to those who have believed in Christ, whether they have made any public profession of their faith, are connected with any church, or have been baptized, or not. Of this class are a part of the Open Communion Baptists and a few Pedobaptists.

All these arguments for an open and unrestricted communion at the Lord's Table, are unsound, and unreasonable, as will appear by a more careful examination of them.

Let us examine in order the positions occupied by these three classes of open communionists.

1st. Those who advocate a free communion, based on the validity of *sprinkling* and *pouring* as modes of baptism, take for granted what is to be proved, namely, that baptism has *several modes*, all equally scriptural. On this point the whole argument rests, whether baptism can be performed in any other way than by immersion? The argument for immersion as the *exclusive* mode of baptism, must determine this question.[1]

2d. Those who assert that a church in admitting persons to the communion should act on the personal convictions of the individual, instead of the settled faith and convictions of the church itself, and receive such as *believe themselves qualified*, whether the church considers them qualified or not.

This mode of reasoning in favor of open communion, is exposed to fatal objections. It denies the right of the church to judge of the fitness of

[1] See Part Second, chap. ii.

candidates to receive the ordinances which it maintains; it allows right of conscience, of judgment, and of action to the *individual*, but denies it to the *church;* it accepts the opinions of persons, rather than the word of God, as the rule of action.

But have churches a right to judge of the qualification of candidates? To say who may, and who may not be admitted to the ordinances of the Gospel? They evidently have such a right. And it is their duty to exercise that right, and to require all who wish to enjoy the privilege, to comply with the conditions of the Gospel—not, indeed, with conditions which they have made, but with those which Christ has established.

Christ has committed the ordinances to his churches for them to preserve in their purity, and to administer in strict fidelity to him; not according to any laws or regulations which the church may create, but according to the laws and conditions which he has given them. If Christ has thrown around the ordinance of the Supper certain conditions as safeguards to its sanctity, it would be a criminal indifference to his authority and disobedience to his commands, to break down those safeguards and allow those conditions to be neglected.

Each church must of necessity be the interpreter of the laws of Christ, so far as its own duties are concerned, just as each individual must be, so far as his duties are concerned. Each church must judge for itself what are the ordinances it is required to administer, and to whom they are to be administered. It would be preposterous to say, that persons outside the church, who had no rights in it, no authority over it, and no connection with it, should dictate to that church and direct whom they should baptize and receive to the Lord's Supper. Or for such persons to come into the church and assert their right to any or all the privileges of the church, without invitation or permission, and even against the wishes and conscientious convictions of its members.

Equally unreasonable would it be for any person outside the church to claim the right to its communion, when he had not complied with the conditions which that church believed the Gospel required. One might as well claim the right to vote in its meetings of business, or exercise any other privilege which belongs to its members alone. It would be no more unreasonable for one to expect to be received to *baptism*, without being *converted*, simply because he thought himself fit, than to expect to be received to *communion* without being *baptized*, simply because he thought himself fit.

If a person can come to the communion on his own convictions, without the consent or against the convictions of the church, he certainly can be received to baptism in the same way. By the same reasoning, he could become a member of the church without the church's act or consent. The supposition is absurd. Such a course would effectually break up and destroy all church order, and the very organization of churches. By this reasoning, also, all discipline would be effectually destroyed ; since, if a church has no right to debar or restrain those outside from its privileges, it certainly has no right to debar or restrain those inside, even when believed to be unworthy ; unless, indeed, the world has more rights and privileges in a Christian church than its own members. Thus, also, a member excluded for heresy, disorderly walk, or vicious conduct, would only be dismissed into a larger liberty, since, as a heathen man and a publican, he could come to the Lord's Table on his own convictions of fitness, while as a *member* he was judged unworthy and denied the privilege. This whole course of reasoning is contradictory, and its conclusions absurd.

No person would expect to enjoy the privileges of membership in any social or secular society, until he had complied with the *conditions* of membership. Much more strictly should the ordinances of the Gospel be guarded and preserved from all infraction, not according to any notions, rules, or prejudices of men, but according to the word and the will of Christ.

3d. Those who deny that baptism is at all necessary as a preparation or qualification for the Lord's Table, substantially deny that the Supper is a memorial of Christ, but hold it only as a sign of Christian fellowship, do violence to Scripture teaching, and contradict the opinions of the great mass of Christians in all ages. They also involve themselves in many difficulties by such an argument.

Is baptism, therefore, *pre-requisite* to the Lord's Supper? Must persons first be baptized in order to have a scriptural right to the communion! Does the New Testament teach this order and relation in the ordinances?

A few deny that baptism is a necessary condition of the Supper, and that few, strange to say, are for the most part Baptists, who attempt to reach an open, or free communion, by this denial. Seeing the logical absurdity of attempting to establish an unrestricted church fellowship with Pedobaptists, while holding baptism to be a prerequisite, they have adopted the theological absurdity of asserting that the inward washing of regeneration was a sufficient, and the only necessary preparation and condition for coming to the Lord's Table, without being baptized at all.

In answer to the views and arguments of this class of persons, consider the following facts:

(*a.*) What are the teachings of the New Testament on this subject? It is very true that neither our Saviour nor his Apostles did, in so many words, declare that no unbaptized person could partake of the Supper. Neither did they say or intimate that unbaptized persons *could* receive the Supper, nor is there the most distant allusion to any such thing. Nor can any part of the New Testament, by the most liberal construction, be made to countenance, or give the least warrant to such an inference. Indeed, these conclusions seem to be reached only by doing violence to the plain and obvious scope and spirit of the inspired teachings.

(*b.*) The example of our Saviour at the institution of the Supper must be observed. Who sat down with him to eat and drink? Whom did he invite to his own table? Unbaptized persons? By no means. But his select and chosen disciples, who had followed him in the regeneration, and were baptized into his name. To these he distributed the symbols of his love and sacrifice.

(*c.*) The language of Christ in the great commission, and in other similar directions and declarations, is against the supposition that unbaptized persons may rightfully receive the Supper. His command is to *teach* all nations, *baptizing* them; declaring that those who *believe*, and are *baptized*, shall be *saved*. The relative order in which these words stand, indicate the relation which the acts they express sustain to each other, and forbid the supposition that persons can lawfully overstep the ordinance of baptism into the most sacred privileges of the church, any more than they can overstep repentance or faith into the ordinance of baptism.

Can it be presumed that Christ would, or that Christian consistency could, put the Lord's Table before either of these injunctions? And if put before "baptize," *where* before? Shall it be before "believe" also, or before "repent?" Who shall determine its true position?

(*d.*) In all the New Testament history, where reference is made to the fellowship of saints in the communion of the Supper, there is not the remotest allusion to the fact that any others were admitted to the privilege except baptized believers. And still more, in all such cases, the circumstances, and the language used, are such as to forbid the inference that unbaptized persons ever received the communion. The directions and instructions of the Apostles with reference to the observance of the Supper, the reproofs administered for an abuse of it, all refer and are addressed exclusively to the members of the churches—baptized believers. These who *believed*, and gladly received the word, were *baptized;* then *added to the church;* and then they continued *steadfast* in the Apostles' *doctrine*, and in *breaking of bread*, and prayer.

(*e.*) The almost universal and unvarying belief and practice of Christian churches and denominations, in all ages, should be regarded as evidence on such a question. Both Catholic and Protestant Christians assert the necessity of baptism as a prerequisite to the Supper.

JUSTIN MARTYR says, "This food is called by us the Eucharist, of which it is not lawful for any to partake but such as believe the things taught by us to be true, and *have been baptized.*"

Dr. WALL says, "No church ever gave the communion to any persons before they were baptized. Among all the absurdities that ever were held, none ever maintained that any person should partake of the communion *before he was baptized.*"

Dr. DODDRIDGE says, "It is certain that so far as our knowledge of primitive antiquity reaches, no *unbaptized* person received the Lord's Supper."

Dr. DICK says, "None having a right to the holy table but those who have been previously purified by the washing of water and by the word."

Indeed, so unanimous and universal have been the opinions and practices of all Christians, in the past, holding baptism to be a condition of, and prerequisite to the communion of the Supper, that the contrary was scarcely thought of, until within a comparatively late period. The splendid talent and genius of Robert Hall gave it an importance never before attained. He wished to practise free communion, and saw no other way of doing it. While holding that *immersion* was the *only* baptism, sprinkled persons could not consistently be invited to the Lord's Table, except by denying that baptism did of necessity precede the Supper. He thrust aside baptism for the sake of reaching his Pedobaptist brethren at the Communion. They accepted his conclusions, were glad to meet him there, but utterly denied his premises, and said that baptism *was* a necessary condition of the communion. Even Mr. Hall saw and acknowledged the difficulties of his position.

His views have obtained considerable favor

with English Baptists, not on account of their consistency or intrinsic force, but because of the great attraction of his reputation and ability. Their want of consistency, however, must prevent their gaining any general prevalence, certainly in this country. Baptists will never accept such arguments, and Pedobaptists will reject a free communion offered on such terms and sustained by such reasoning.

III.—Baptists' Communion.

The view which Baptists take of the Lord's Supper is this: that it is a symbolic ordinance, designed to set forth and teach great practical and fundamental doctrines in the Gospel economy; that it is an ordinance of commemoration, observed, not as a test of Christian fellowship, but in remembrance of Christ; that the church has both the right and is in duty bound to judge of the fitness of candidates to partake of it, strictly guarding its sanctity from all unlawful intrusion; and that baptism—that is, *immersion*, in the name of the Father, Son, and Holy Spirit, on a profession of faith in Christ—is prerequisite to it.

Baptism, though it must necessarily precede the Supper, is not, however, the only condition on which the privileges of the communion depend.

What, then, are these conditions or *prerequisites* to the communion? They are three: 1. *Conversion;* 2. *Baptism;* 3. *A godly life.* A church is not at liberty to require less nor more of any one than this.

1. *Conversion.*—No person has any right to, nor can be a suitable subject for the privileges of the communion, unless he is truly regenerated by the Spirit of God, having exercised a saving faith in Christ. Even though he may have been baptized, and may be living an upright life, without regeneration he cannot be a spiritual member of Christ, and consequently not a fit member of his church.

2. *Baptism.*—By this ordinance a Christian disciple is transferred from the world and initiated into the church. As the Supper is an ordinance within the church, the individual must pass through this door of baptism to reach it. By the regenerating work of the Spirit on the heart, one becomes a member of Christ's spiritual body, so by a confession and a symbolic representation of that inward work in the ordinance of baptism, he becomes a member of the visible church. Without scriptural baptism, therefore, one cannot properly be a member of the church, nor entitled to the communion.

3. *A godly life.*—A person may have been

truly converted and scripturally baptized, and yet, if he has imbibed dangerous heresies, or if he be living in the practice of grievous sins, or otherwise *walking disorderly*, so as to be a reproach to his profession and an injury to the cause of Gospel truth, he is not a fit subject for the sacred privileges of the Lord's Supper. His walk and conversation must be such as become godliness, and as will not dishonor the Gospel he professes to obey.

It is, therefore, abundantly evident that the ordinance of the Supper is, in the strictest sense, a *church* ordinance; that is, to be administered within the church, and to those within the church. The church is also to judge of the qualifications of those who wish to receive it, and to decide who has, and who has not complied with the Gospel conditions.

This statement of the *three prerequisites* to communion sufficiently explains the *three* following *facts*.

(*a*.) The reason why Baptists do not invite Pedobaptists to their communion, is because such persons have not been baptized. And even though *they say* and *think* they have been baptized, yet the church with which they may desire to commune must judge of that question in the case of all who propose to partake with them.

Persons only *sprinkled*, or *poured upon*, are not scripturally baptized, and therefore cannot consistently be invited to the Supper in a church where nothing but *immersion* is believed to be baptism.

(*b*.) The reason why Baptists do not feel at liberty to commune with Pedobaptists is the same, viz.: they do not consider such persons as baptized at all. They would be giving their example and influence to sanction and support what they believe to be an error, should they commune with such, however pious and godly in other respects they might be.

(*c*.) The reason why Baptist churches do not invite *immersed members* of Pedobaptist churches to their communion is, because such persons, though they have been scripturally baptized, yet, by continuing in a church which practises sprinkling for baptism, thus putting a human device in place of an ordinance of Christ, they are thereby *walking disorderly* as to Gospel truth and Gospel ordinances, and are not entitled to the privilege of the Supper. This is the more obvious, because such persons believe that sprinkling is not scriptural baptism, inasmuch as they would not receive it for baptism, but were immersed. By continuing their membership in such a church, therefore, they are supporting what they themselves believe and confess to be an error. For this reason, Baptists do properly refuse them an invitation to the Lord's Table.

IV.—Pedobaptist Communion.

Pedobaptist churches believe in, and practise close communion as *really*, though not to the same extent, as do the Baptists. And all such churches admit, and profess to be governed by the same rules and principles, as to the *terms* and *subjects* of communion, as do Baptist churches themselves; the same as are set forth above. The real difference is in their views of baptism.

These churches, whether they be Congregationalists, Episcopalian, Methodist, Presbyterian, or of any other evangelical denomination, agree entirely with the Baptists, that persons must receive baptism *before* being admitted to the Supper. Nor will they allow any, though they be their dearest friends, and acknowledged to be truly regenerate and living godly lives, to come to the communion until they have been baptized, as *they*—that is, the *church*, not the *individual*—understand baptism, either by *sprinkling*, *pouring*, or *dipping*. All others they exclude from the Lord's Table, thereby practising close communion.

Now, for the communion to be really *open*, the church must impose *no conditions*, must require no qualifications, but leave it entirely to the choice of the individual, to partake or not, as he may please, and according as his personal wish, or sense of propriety, may dictate. The moment a church says, the person must be baptized, or converted even, or must comply with any other condition, that moment it *restricts* the communion to a specific class, shutting out all others, and of necessity it becomes a restricted, or *close* communion. This result is inevitable.

All churches that claim the right to judge of the fitness of persons who receive the Supper, and admit only those who have complied with certain conditions as prerequisites, excluding all others, are truly and properly close communion. And those only are truly and properly open communion, which allow all persons to be judges, each in his own case, of his fitness for the ordinance, and to receive it if he desires to do so.

Baptists and Pedobaptists agree as to the relations of the ordinances, and as to the terms of communion, but differ as to what baptism is; or rather, as to how it is to be administered. Baptists assert that *dipping* is its *only* mode, while

Pedobaptists declare that it may properly be administered by *dipping*, *pouring*, or *sprinkling*. They all agree that baptism is a prerequisite to the communion; consequently, that no person, however good and holy, has a right to the latter until he has received the former. They all agree further, that the church which spreads the Supper, is to judge whether those who desire to come to it are qualified, by having complied with the conditions.

It is true, Baptists carry their close communion one step further than Pedobaptists do, by excluding *them* from the Supper, as they exclude others, but for the same reason, and by the same rule. The difference between them consists in their different views of what constitutes baptism. Pedobaptists are therefore most unreasonable, who say they do not object to Baptists' views of baptism, but dislike their close communion; whereas, the real difficulty is with baptism. If their views of baptism are correct, their close communion follows of necessity, even according to the reasoning and practice of Pedobaptists themselves. All follow the same rule as to the Supper. They should, therefore, first prove that immersion is not the only mode of baptism taught in the New Testament, or cease their objection to close communion as practised by Baptists.

It must not be overlooked, also, that in one direction, Pedobaptists carry their practice of close communion much further than the Baptists do; inasmuch as they exclude from the Lord's Table a large class of their own members, viz., *baptized children*, not allowing them communion, though they be members. Baptists do not deny the Supper to their own members, in good standing. If children are suitable subjects for baptism, it seems most unreasonable to exclude them from the communion.

V.—Objections Answered.

Various *objections* are urged by Pedobaptists against the views and practices of Baptists respecting the Communion.

1. Baptists are sometimes asked by Pedobaptists, "Why do you not invite us to your communion? Is it because you do not consider us Christians?"

To this, the simple answer is, Because you have not been baptized. And Baptists might inquire in return, Why do you not invite to your communion persons converted but not baptized? Are they not Christians? If Christ has received them, why do you reject them?

2. Again it is said, "Baptism is not a *saving*

ordinance; why, then, make it a test of communion?"

To this the answer is, Why do you make baptism a test of communion, by refusing to commune with those whom you say have not been baptized? But, shall we refuse to obey Christ unless it be in something which we consider *saving?* Shall we disregard plain positive commands, because we dislike them? Baptists do not practise immersion because it is *saving*, but because it is *commanded.* They do not baptize candidates to save them; but to show that they are already saved; that is, in a state of grace or salvation. Those who recognize Christ as their only lawgiver in matters of religion, should not presume to question the propriety, or decide as to the importance of his commands. Their duty is to *obey.*

3. Or the objection may be urged in this form, "You make too much of baptism; you make it a *saving* ordinance."

To this objection, this is the reply: We do not make it a saving ordinance, because we will not administer it to persons until after they have exercised a saving faith in Christ. They are, therefore, *saved* before we will baptize them. You are the ones who make baptism a saving ordinance, by administering it to unconscious infants before they can exercise repentance or a saving faith, believing that in some mysterious way their salvation is more probable, than if not baptized, and consequently believing that baptism has a sanctifying, or a saving efficacy, on those to whom it is administered.

4. It is also said, "We invite you to our communion; why do you not show the same liberal and generous spirit?"

To which they reply, You can well afford to invite us, and do no violence to your conscience, because you believe that *our* baptism is scriptural and valid. But since we do not believe that *your* baptism is either scriptural or valid, we cannot invite you to the Lord's Table without doing what we believe to be contrary to the Gospel, thereby violating our consciences.

5. Some urge this objection, "It is the Lord's Table, why, therefore, do you exclude any of the Lord's people?"

A sufficient answer is to say, It *is* the *Lord's* Table, therefore we have no discretion in the case. We have no right to do less or more than he has commanded. If it were *our* table, we might invite all. But we must not love our brethren better than we love Christ. We must not be so anxious to please and commune with the disciples, as to disobey the Master for the sake of doing it. Because it is the Lord's Table, we cannot go beyond his instructions. We must be guided not by sympathies for our brethren, but by love for our Lord: that love which *obeys.*

6. Sometimes it is said, "If the Lord has received us, why should not you?"

This supposes that all whom the Lord receives to a spiritual fellowship with himself, in the forgiveness of sins, the church ought to receive to its communion. If this be so, then ought Pedobaptists to receive unbaptized converts to their communion. But this is an error. The Lord receives children dying in unconscious infancy; but that is no reason why the church should administer the Supper to such.

7. Again, this objection is urged, "We hope to commune together in heaven, ought we not, therefore, to commune together on earth?"

This, like most other similar objections, is probably made more for the sake of objecting than because it has any force against what is called "close communion." It is based on a misconception of the true nature of Christ's temporal kingdom, and the distinction between the earthly and the heavenly states of the church. It supposes that we should invite to the Lord's Table all with whom we hope to commune in heaven. If this be true, then Pedobaptists are doing wrong as well as Baptists. But this, also, is an error. We all *hope* to meet many from among papists, heretics, and perhaps heathen, many even who are now unconverted, in heaven. But is that any reason why we should invite them to the fellowship of the church now? Certainly not. Christ has given his church laws, regulations, offices, and ordinances, to fit it for its work, and meet the conditions of its earthly state, none of which will be had or needed in the heavenly state.

8. Baptists are sometimes accused of being "bigoted," "unkind," "sectarian," "thinking themselves better than others," "opposed to Christian union," because they practise a restricted communion.

The same charge might be brought with equal force against Pedobaptists, since they also practise a restricted communion. But how can these charges be made against those who are simply and only attempting to do what they conscientiously believe the law of Christ requires them to do? If they are mistaken, show them their error. They have no love for, nor profit in close communion, aside from their desire to obey Christ. They believe and practise it under great temporal disadvantages, bearing the censures of their brethren on account of it. Their only attachment to it or interest in it, arises from the fact that they believe it to be according to the will and the word of Christ, and they desire to be found obeying the divine requisition. Prove to them that *sprinkling* is enjoined in the New Testament, for baptism, or that *unbaptized persons* should be admitted to the Lord's Supper, and they will abandon restricted communion. Until this is done, all unkind censures, for doing what they believe to be right, appear very much as if those who make them, have a secret conviction that they themselves are the ones in error, which unpleasant conviction they wish to hide by objecting to others.

Let every one who professes to love Christ, endeavor to maintain a spirit of humility and meekness, being gentle and kind to all, never accusing, ever forgiving; by careful study of God's word, and prayer for the illumination of the Holy Spirit, seeking to know what the Divine Truth teaches, and what the will of God is, and allowing no human influence to prevent a strict obedience to God's word, in all things.

CHAPTER V.

THE QUESTION OF CHURCH OFFICERS.

How many orders of *officers* ought a church to have, according to the teachings of the New Testament and the practice of the Apostles and early Christians?

Baptists, and some other denominations of Christians, say there are, and ought to be *two* only. These two are *pastors* and *deacons*. But some denominations say there ought to be *three* orders in the ministry, and the Romish Church has carried the number up to ten or twelve.

In the New Testament the word *bishop*, or *pastor*, and *presbyter*, or *elder*, imply the same office, and are frequently applied to the same individual.[1] The *bishop* was the *pastor*, or *overseer* of the church. The *deacons* were chosen to attend rather to the temporal affairs of the church, and thereby allow the pastor, or bishop, to devote himself more exclusively to its spiritual interests.

NEANDER says, the word *presbyter*, or *elder*,

[1] See First Part, chap. ii. and vii.

indicated rather the dignity of the office, since presbyters among the Jews were usually aged and venerable men, while *bishop* or *episcopos* designated the nature of their work, as overseers, or pastors of the churches. The former title was used by Jewish Christians, as a name familiar in the synagogue, while the latter was chiefly used by the Greek and other Gentile converts, as more familiar and expressive to them.

The *bishops*, *presbyters*, *pastors*, or by whatever other name they might be called, were *equal* in authority and the dignity of their office. There was no high order of the clergy, placed over other and lower orders, as is now seen in some churches. But in process of time, as young or feeble churches grew up near, or arose out of those older and stronger, gradually the pastors of the older and stronger ones, secured an ascendency over the feebler; and the older churches themselves obtained a controlling power over the younger. Thus arose the rule of the metropolitan over the provincial churches, and the higher clergy over the lower, and the multiplication of orders in the ministry.

This departure from apostolic practice was natural, though not scriptural, is easily traced in history, and generally conceded by scholars and historians.

In the Epistles of Paul, the titles *presbyter* or *elder*, and *episcopos* or *bishop*, are used interchangeably, and often addressed to the same individual, and the qualifications and duties of both are the same. This goes to prove that they were one and the same office and officer. Pastors and deacons are therefore the only scriptural officers in a Gospel church. With these views entirely agree many eminent Christian writers, both ancient and modern, a great part of whom are staunch prelatists themselves, as Bernaldus, Isidorus, Theodoret, Chrysostom, Jerome, Whittaker, and Usher.

CHAPTER VI.

THE QUESTION OF CHURCH GOVERNMENT.

WHAT is the true scriptural form of *church government?*[1] How ought churches to be governed, and by whom should their affairs be administered?

There are *three* principal forms of church government practised. 1. The *prelatical ;* where the governing power resides in prelates, or bishops, as in the Romish, Greek, English, and some other churches. 2. The *presbyterian;* where the governing power resides in presbyteries and synods, as in the Scotch Kirk, the Lutheran, and the various Presbyterian churches. 3. The *independent;* where the governing power resides in the members of each individual church, as the Baptists, Congregationalists, and some others. Which of these best accords with the understood constitution and government of the apostolic churches?

Each Baptist church is distinct from, and inde-

[1] See First Part, chap. vi.

pendent of all others, having no ecclesiastical connection with any, though maintaining a friendly Christian intercourse with all. The government is administered by the body of the members, where no one possesses a preëminence, but each enjoys an equality of rights. This, they assert, is according to the Gospel idea, and the practice of the primitive churches, and the teachings of the New Testament.

To confirm this view, it will be found that the Apostles regarded and treated the churches as independent bodies. They directed their epistles to the *churches* as such, and addressed the members as equals among themselves. They reported their own doings to the churches, and enjoined upon them the duty of discipline. They also recognized the right of the churches to elect their own officers.

MOSHEIM declares: "The power of enacting laws, of appointing teachers and ministers, and of determining controversies, was lodged in the people at large."

NEANDER says: "The churches were taught to govern themselves. The brethren chose their own officers from among themselves." With these views agree many other able scholars and historians.

MOSHEIM describes the primitive church thus:

"Each independent church, which had a bishop or presbyter of its own, assumed to itself the forms and rights of a little republic, or commonwealth." Dr. Barrows, Dr. Burton, Archbishop Whately, with other prelatists, agree in this opinion, as likewise do nearly all reliable authorities on the history and constitution of the primitive church.

In this respect, therefore, Baptist churches are unquestionably founded on the apostolic model.

CHAPTER VII.

BAPTIST HISTORY.

THE question is often asked by persons not acquainted with Baptist history, "Where did the Baptists originate?" "How old are they?" "Who were their founders?" Really it is not so important to know when, or how a denomination originated, as to know whether they believe and practise according to the Gospel. All that is old is not true; nor is it any evidence that a church is scriptural because it has antiquity to boast. A glance at Baptist history may not be unprofitable, however.

1. *Early Sects.*

It is conceded by all who are at all familiar with history, that from the days of the Apostles to the present time, there have existed companies, congregations, and sects of Christians, separate from the prevailing state churches. As soon as such prevailing churches fell into errors, became proud, corrupt, and worldly, departing from the simplicity and spirituality of the Gospel, then such as continued spiritual and godly separated themselves from the multitude, worshipped by themselves, and served God according to the dictates of their own consciences. They maintained the doctrines and ordinances of Christ as he had delivered them to his disciples, and were his true and faithful witnesses.

During all the world's dark ages, since the kingdom of Christ appeared, these sects and companies are admitted to have existed. They have been called by many names, and have differed somewhat among themselves in different ages and in different countries. By the prevailing churches from whom they were separated, they have been called *heretics*, have been defamed, and persecuted perpetually. Thousands on thousands of them have been put to death by the most painful tortures, while those spared to live have been afflicted by unequalled cruelties. Emperors, kings, and rulers, popes, priests, and bishops, senates, synods, and councils, have persecuted them with every device which malice could invent or power execute, to waste, blot out, and exterminate them from the earth.

They were the few among the many, the weak oppressed by the strong; with none to plead their cause or to defend their rights, they could do nothing but suffer. Though calumniated by their enemies, who accused them of every crime, and charged them with every enormity, they were the purest and the best of the ages and the countries in which they lived, and maintained the ordinances and doctrines of the Gospel nearly in their primitive purity. Many of them had separated themselves from the prevailing churches to find a purer worship elsewhere, while the greater part had never been connected with the Romish hierarchy.

Like some rivulet which pursues its way from the mountains to the sea, parallel to, but never mingling with the broad and turbulent stream, these people have come down from the first ages of Christianity, preserving and transmitting to posterity the purest forms of practical godliness and Gospel faith known to history during those long-succeeding centuries of darkness and corruption. The reproaches and persecutions they suffered were because they bore testimony against the errors and crimes that were practised in the name of religion. No doubt they had some faults, and maintained some errors; but these were fewer by far than those of their enemies.

During the *two first* centuries, Messalians, Euchites, Montanists, were the names by which some of these sects were known.

In the *third*, *fourth*, and *fifth* centuries, the Novatians arose, and became exceedingly numerous, spreading throughout the Roman empire, notwithstanding the persecutions practised upon them by their enemies.

Then came, in the *fourth* century, also the Donatists, who multiplied rapidly, spread far and wide, and continued long to exist.

In the *seventh* century the Paulicians began to attract public attention, and long continued, with others, the objects of hatred and persecution by the Romish church.

All these professed to hold the New Testament as the only rule of faith and practice, and to live by its teachings. They held that none ought to be received to membership in the churches, except persons truly regenerated. They rebaptized those received among them from the Romish Church, and for doing so were called *Anabaptists.* They rejected infant baptism, as Mosheim, Allix, Robinson, and other historians assert. They baptized by immersion, as did all professing Christians during those ages.[1] Robinson, the historian, calls them "Trinitarian Baptists." The Paulicians became exceedingly numerous, and were so cruelly persecuted that the empress

[1] See Part Second, chap. ii. 4, 5.

Theodora is said to have caused not less than *one hundred thousand* to be put to death, having first confiscated their property.

About the close of the *tenth* century came into notice the Paterines, who probably were substantially the same people as those previously existing under other names. These also rejected infant baptism, protested against the corruptions of the Romish Church, and, in consequence, experienced severe and long-continued persecution from it.

In the *eleventh* and following centuries, these sects took new names, and attracted new attention through Europe. They were called, Waldenses, Albigenses, Vaudois, Cathari, Poor Men of Lyons.. They became very numerous, and for centuries continued to multiply, and to suffer persecution.

All these ancient sects, though not known by the name of *Baptists*, did hold the prevailing opinions which now characterize the Baptists. As, for instance, they asserted the rights of faith and conscience; rejecting the authority of popes, and the interference of princes in matters of religion; they denied infant baptism; they baptized by dipping; they declared the Bible to be the only rule of faith and practice in matters of religion; and admitted none to their churches except regenerated and godly persons. They differed somewhat among themselves in different countries and in different times, which was natural, as they had no general ecclesiastical organization, but existed in independent churches and communities, constantly harassed, persecuted, and scattered by their enemies.

From the apostolic age to the Reformation these people were the purest and the best the world had to boast. They were the true church and people of God. At the time of the Reformation, under Luther, these sects, to a great degree, fraternized with, and were lost in the multitudes of the reformers. Those that continued a separate existence, as the Waldenses of Piedmont, abandoned dipping, adopted infant baptism, and took the general forms of faith and worship adopted by Protestant Pedobaptists.

2. *Dutch Baptists.*

The Baptists of Holland are acknowledged by historians to have had their origin at a very remote period. MOSHEIM says: "The true origin of that sect which acquired the name of Anabaptists, *is hid in the remote depths of antiquity*, and is consequently extremely difficult to be ascertained."[1] ZUINGLE, the Swiss reformer, con-

[1] Maclain's translation, edition 1811.

temporary with Luther, says: "The institution of Anabaptism is no novelty, but for *thirteen hundred years* has caused great disturbance in the church." If it had existed 1,300 years before Zuingle, it must have gone back to within two hundred years of Christ, to say the least.

Dr. DERMONT, chaplain to the King of Holland, and Dr. YPEIJ, theological professor at Groningen, received, a few years since, a royal commission to prepare a history of the Reformed Dutch Church. That history contains the following manly, generous, and truthful testimony touching the Dutch Baptists: "We have now seen that the Baptists, who were formerly called Anabaptists, and in later times Mennonites, were the original Waldenses, and have long in the history of the church received the honor of that origin. *On this account the Baptists may be considered the only Christian community which has stood since the apostles, and as a Christian society, which has preserved pure the doctrines of the Gospel through all ages.*"

This is earnest and reliable testimony from those who are not Baptists, and who have no personal sympathy with the Baptists, but who speak frankly the truths which history has recorded.

3. *Welsh Baptists.*

The Welsh Baptists claim their origin direct from the Apostles, and urge in favor of the claim reasons so cogent as have never been disproved. When Austin, the Romish monk, visited Wales about the close of the *sixth century*, he found a community of more than *two thousand* Christians living quietly in the mountains, who discarded the authority of the Romish Church. Austin labored to bring them to what he considered the true faith. They refused all his overtures. Yielding things in general, he reduced his demand to three things in particular, namely, *First*, that they should observe Easter in due form, as ordered by the church. *Second*, That they should give christendom, or baptism, to their children. *Third*, That they should preach to the English the word of God, as formerly directed.

This demand upon them proves that they neither observed the Romish ordinance of Easter, nor baptized their children. Nor would they submit to this final demand; whereupon Austin threatened them with war and wretchedness. Not long after, Wales was invaded by the Saxons, and many of these Christians cruelly murdered—as was believed—at the instigation of the exacting and bigoted Austin.

4. *English Baptists.*

In England, from the *twelfth* to the *seventeenth century*, many Baptists suffered cruel persecutions and death, by burning, drowning, beheading, with many inhuman tortures, because they worshipped God according to the dictates of His word and their own consciences, and refused to submit their faith to the dictates of popes and kings.

In 1538, royal edicts were issued against them, and several were burnt in Smithfield. Brandt writes that, "In the year 1538, thirty-one Baptists that fled from England, were put to death at Deft, in Holland; the men were beheaded, and the women drowned." Bishop Latimer declares, that "Baptists were burned in different parts of the kingdom, and went to death with good integrity," during the time of Edward VI. Under the rule of the Popish Mary, they suffered, perhaps, no more than under that of the Protestant Elizabeth: for during the reign of the latter, a congregation of Baptists being discovered in London, some were banished, twenty-seven imprisoned, and two burnt at Smithfield. In 1639, Bailey wrote, that "under the shadow of independency, they have lifted up their heads, and increased their numbers above all sects in the land. They have forty-six churches in and about London. They are a people very fond of religious liberty, and very unwilling to be brought under bondage of the judgment of any other."

5. *American Baptists.*

The history of American Baptists goes back somewhat more than *two hundred years.* At what time they first came to the country it is impossible to say. The first church was organized at Providence, R. I., under the care of Roger Williams, 1639. Mr. Williams was born in Wales in 1598, educated at Oxford, England, and in 1630 came to America, and was minister of the Puritan Church at Salem, Mass. But soon after, having adopted Baptist sentiments, he was banished and driven out of Massachusetts. After having endured many and severe sufferings in consequence, he settled at Providence, with a few followers of like faith, laid the foundations of that city, and having procured a charter for the new colony, became the founder of Rhode Island, calling both the State and city *Providence*, in recognition of the divine guidance and protection which he had experienced.

Mr. Williams was the first governor of the colony, as well as first pastor of the church. He gave *free toleration* in matters of religious faith and practice to all who chose to settle with him. Thus he became the first ruler, and Rhode Island the first State which offered entire liberty to every person to worship God according to their own choice, without interference from the civil authority. As there was no Baptist minister in the colony, now accessible, Mr. Williams was immersed by one of his associates, a layman, when he in turn baptized his associates, and organized a church 1639. On account of the toleration granted to all, other Baptists, who suffered much elsewhere, collected at Providence, and at an early period spread through the colony.

The next church formed was in Newport, in 1644. There is, however, a considerable controversy as to whether the present first church in Providence, or the first church in Newport, is the older. Priority is claimed by both.

Several of the churches formed next in order of time were as follows: second church, Newport, R.I., 1656; first, Swansea, Mass., 1663; first, Boston, 1665; church, North Kingston, R.I., 1665; Seventh-day church, Newport, 1671; church, South Kingston, R.I., 1680; church, Tiverton, R.I., 1685; church, Middletown, N.J., 1688; church, Dublin, Pa., 1689; church, Piscataway, N.J., 1689; church, Charleston, S.C., 1690; church, Cohansey, N.J., 1691; second church, Swansea, 1693; church, Philadelphia, Pa., 1698; church, Welsh Tract, Del., 1701; church, Groton, Ct., 1705; church, Smithfield, R.I., 1706; Seventh-day church, Piscataway, 1707; church, Hopkinton, R.I., 1708.

In the common course of emigration, and the usual changes of society, the sentiments of the Baptists spread and their churches multiplied. In 1768, there were, according to Edward's Tables, 137 churches in America. In 1790, according to Asplund's Register, there were 872 churches; 722 ordained and 449 unordained ministers; with 64,975 church members. In 1812, according to Benedict's History, the number of churches was 2,633; ordained ministers, 2,142; associations, 111; and 204,185 church members. In 1836, according to Allen's Triennial Register, there were 372 associations; 7,299 churches; 4,075 ordained and 966 licensed ministers; 517,523 church members, including the small denominations of Seventh-day, Six Principle, and Free-will Baptists.[1]

[1] Much of the above information and statistics has been obtained from Benedict's History of the Baptists, in which may be found a vast amount of facts and history relating to the Baptists, both American and foreign, ancient and modern.

It has been by some supposed, that all the Baptist churches in the United States originated in, and grew out of, that which Roger Williams founded. This is a great mistake. Other churches grew up in rapid succession around it, but having no connection with it; being composed either of immigrants from Europe, or of converts gathered on the ground.

It is estimated that one quarter of the population of the United States is connected with the Baptist denomination; nearly one quarter with the Methodists; the remainder being divided among the various other denominations. The Baptists represent a large amount of wealth, but not so much in proportion to their numbers as several of the other denominations.

The subjoined Table is taken from the Baptist Almanac, published by the American Baptist Publication Society, for 1859, which gives the statistics for each State, for the United States, and for North America, together with those of the several smaller Baptist denominations. It must be remembered, however, that these estimates fall considerably below the truth, since there are many churches not connected with the Associations, as well as many of the associated churches, from which no reports are obtained.

REGULAR BAPTISTS IN NORTH AMERICA.

STATES.	Associations	Churches.	Ordained Ministers.	Licentiates.	Baptized in 1857.	Total Num.
Alabama,	27	709	362	58	3,917	52,696
Arkansas,	16	255	117	6	971	8,704
California,	1	19	14	2	52	932
Connecticut,	7	118	114	18	598	16,308
Delaware,	...	2	8	....	5	379
District of Columbia,	...	4	7	5	100	930
Florida,	3	100	46	20	318	4,396
Georgia,	37	905	538	158	6,015	72.160
Illinois,	34	602	413	64	2,482	31,448
Indiana,	47	606	290	44	2,132	29,756
Indian Territory,	4	40	88	....	3[illegible]1	4.050
Iowa,	10	167	124	26	718	7,561
Kentucky,	44	897	396	40	5,118	78,972
Louisiana,	9	176	85	6	873	8,765
Maine,	13	276	185	12	757	18,530
Maryland,	1	32	24	7	599	3,834
Massachusetts,	14	257	267	18	1,745	33.205
Michigan,	11	186	126	11	602	9,924
Minnesota,	2	31	28	2	60	818
Mississippi,	21	561	269	38	2,614	36,123
Missouri,	32	6[illegible]9	359	49	2,897	37,076
New Hampshire,	7	91	79	7	262	7.777
New Jersey,	4	114	115	18	845	14,846
New York,	43	812	738	90	4,326	84 266
North Carolina,	27	645	348	71	4,244	52,275
Ohio,	29	474	3[illegible]4	39	1,928	27,389
Oregon,	2	27	16	6	116	877
Pennsylvania,	16	369	259	55	2,093	33,753
Rhode Island	2	50	56	7	290	7,582
South Carolina,	17	451	267	23	4,776	54.278
Tennessee,	25	655	381	55	3,124	50,539
Texas,	15	821	161	18	1,463	12,822
Vermont,	7	105	89	3	267	7.481
Virginia	26	7[illegible]4	360	43	5,794	102,667
Wisconsin,	7	153	86	...	421	6,379
German and Dutch Ch. in the U. S.	1	40	30	11	263	2,000
*Swedish Churches in the U. S.	1	8	7	....	130	400
*Welsh Churches in the U. S.	3	84	20	....	240	1,300
Total in the United States,	565	11,600	7,141	1,025	63,506	923,198
*British Provinces,	13	350	212	....	1,700	29,200
*West Indies,	4	110	125	38	1,800	36,250
Total in North America,	582	12,060	7,478	1,063	67,006	988,648

* Estimated.

OTHER DENOMINATIONS THAT PRACTISE IMMERSION.

	Associations	Churches.	Ordained Ministers.	Licentiates.	Baptized in 1857.	Total Num.
Anti-Mission Baptists in the U. S...	155	1,720	825	....	1,500	58,000
Free-Will Baptists,..............	180	1,170	945	143	1,415	50,312
Six Principle Baptists,............	...	18	16	....	.....	8,000
Seventh-Day Baptists,............	...	67	70	17	.....	7,250
Church of God,..................	...	275	132	....	.....	13,800
*Disciples,......................	...	2,000	2,000	....	.....	350,000
Tunkers,........................	...	150	200	....	.....	8,200
Mennonites, ...	...	800	250	....	.....	36,280

INCREASE IN TEN YEARS.

The following is the rate of progress made in the Regular Baptist Churches in the United States during the last ten years, from 1848 to 1858:

	Associations.	Churches.	Ordained Ministers.	Members
1858............	565	11,600	7,141	923,198
1848............	421	8,205	4,950	667,750
Increase,.......	144	3,395	2,191	255,448

OTHER FACTS.

From the same source of information, it appears that in all churches practising immersion, there has been an increase of *immersed believers*, in *ten years*, of 475,878, being an average of 47,587 each year. Besides these, many are yearly immersed in the various Pedobaptist churches.

* This we regard as a very high estimate, but the figures were the result of inquiry of one of the most careful and reliable ministers of the denomination to which they refer.

There are more than *thirty weekly religious periodicals*, among the Baptists in the United States, with *fourteen monthly*, and *two quarterly* publications.

As to institutions of learning, there are *thirty-four colleges* and *twelve theological seminaries*, besides other less important schools.

BAPTISTS IN ENGLAND.

From the Baptist Manual for 1858, published in London, we learn, that in Great Britain and Ireland, there are 33 Baptist Associations, 1917 churches, and 101,397 church members, with 137,524 Sunday-school scholars. During the year, 23 new church edifices were erected, 8 old ones enlarged, and 13 new churches constituted. The denomination has 5 institutions of learning for the training of young men for the ministry. Their Foreign Mission Society sustains missions in the East and West Indies, Africa, Australia, Central America, and on the European Continent; while its receipts amount to $115,000 annually. The denomination is rapidly increasing in numbers, influence, and public esteem.

CHAPTER VIII.

FORMS AND BLANKS.

THERE is no fixed and necessary form for Letters of Dismission, Minutes of Councils, Conventions, and the like. They will vary according to the customs of churches and the taste of those who construct them. The following present substantially the forms in common use:

1. *Letter of Dismission.*[1]

The —— Baptist Church of ————

To the —— Baptist Church of ————.

DEAR BRETHREN:

This is to certify that ——— ——— is a member in good and regular standing with us, and at —— own request is hereby dismissed for the purpose of uniting with you. When —— has so united, —— connection with us will cease.

Done by order of the Church.

NEW York, *May* ——, 18—.

——— ———, *Ch. Clerk.*

This letter will be valid for —— months.

[1] See First Part, chap. viii., iii., 1.

NOTE.—It is customary to limit letters to a specified time. If they are not used during that time, an explanation must be given to the church which granted them. The letters can be renewed at the discretion of the church.

---

2. *Letter of Commendation.*

NEW YORK, *May* ——, 18—.

This certifies that —— —— is a member in good standing in the —— Baptist Church in ——, and is hereby commended to the confidence and fellowship of sister churches, wherever Providence may direct.

—— ——,
Pastor —— Baptist Church.

NOTE.—This form of letter is for members during a temporary absence from home, and given either by the pastor or by the church.

---

3. *Letter of Notification.*

NEW YORK, *May* ——, 18—.

To the —— Baptist Church.

DEAR BRETHREN:

This certifies that —— —— was received by letter from you, to membership in the —— Baptist Church, May ——, 18—.

—— ——, *Ch. Clerk.*

NOTE 1.—This form is by some churches attached to every letter of dismission granted, and is to be filled by the church receiving said letter, and returned to notify the church granting it, that the member has been admitted to their fellowship.

NOTE 2.—Sometimes a letter is granted to "any church of the same faith and order," instead of to a specified church, in cases where the member is not certain with what church he may wish to unite.

NOTE 3.—When members are dismissed to constitute a new church, that fact should be stated in the letter.

4. *Minutes of Church Meeting.*

NEW YORK, *May* ——, 18—.

The church held its regular meeting for business this evening, at —— o'clock. Pastor, moderator.

After singing, and reading the Scriptures, prayer was offered by ——— ———.

Minutes of the last meeting were read and approved.

[Then follows a faithful record of the business transacted.]

Meeting adjourned.

——— ———, *Clerk.*

NOTE.—The records of a church should show, not only the bare minutes of its business, but a concise and comprehensive history of its progress, embracing all the important changes, incidents, and events which transpire in connection with it.

5. *Call for an Ordaining Council.*

NEW YORK, *May* ——, 18—.

The —— Baptist Church of ————

To the —— Baptist Church of ————

DEAR BRETHREN:

You are requested to send your pastor and two brethren, to sit in council with us, July ——, at —— o'clock, to consider the propriety of publicly setting apart to the work of the Gospel ministry, our brother ——— ———.

The Council will meet in . . . .

The following churches are invited: . . . .

By order of the Church,

——— ———. *Clerk.*

---

6. *Call for a Recognizing Council.*

NEW YORK, *May* ——, 18—.

To the —— Baptist Church in ————.

DEAR BRETHREN:

In behalf of a company of brethren and sisters in Christ, you are requested to send your pastor and two delegates, to meet in council at ———, July ——, at —— o'clock, to consider the propriety of recognizing said company of brethren and sisters, as a regular and independent Church of Christ.

The following churches are invited: . . .
. . . .

Affectionately yours, etc.,

—— ——,

Com. or Clerk.

---

7. *Call for an Advisory Council.*

New York, *May* ——, 18—.

The —— Baptist Church,

To the Baptist Church of ———

Dear Brethren:

You are requested to send your pastor and two delegates, to sit in council July ——, 18—, at —— o'clock, to advise with us concerning certain unhappy difficulties existing among us, which are disturbing our peace, and threatening the most serious consequences to the welfare of the church.[1]

The council will be held at ———. The following churches are invited: . . . . . .

By order of the Church,

—— —— *Clerk.*

[1] See First Part, chap xii. 1.

NOTE 1.—An advisory council may be called by *individuals* or by a *church.* It may also be called to give advice as to other matters, than those which disturb the peace and harmony of the church.

NOTE 2.—The form of the call should indicate the object of the council, and the churches invited.

---

8. *Minutes of a Council.*

NEW YORK, *May* ——, 18—

An ecclesiastical council, called by the ——— church, convened at ——— this day, at ——— o'clock.

Organized by choosing ——— ——— Moderator, and ——— ——— Clerk.

Prayer was offered by ——— ———.

The records of the church, relating to the call of this council were read, stating the object to be . . . .

The credentials of delegates were presented. The following churches were represented by the following brethren:

Churches.	*Delegates.*
———	———
———	———
———	———

[Then follows a faithful record of whatever business is done.]

Council dissolved.

——— ——— *Moderator.*

——— ——— *Clerk.*

NOTE 1.—A true and faithful record of the proceedings of the council is to be made by the clerk, read and approved by the council at the close, and signed by the moderator and clerk.

NOTE 2.—A copy of the minutes duly certified and signed, should be furnished to the church, or persons calling the council.

---

9. *Minutes of Committee.*

NEW YORK, *May*, 18—

——— Committee met at ——— at —— o'clock.

Present, ...

Brother ——— ——— in the chair.

Prayer by ——— ———.

Minutes of last meeting read and approved.

[Record of business.]

Adjourned.

——— ——— *Secretary.*

---

10. *Minutes of a Convention.*

NEW YORK, *May*, — 18—

A convention called to consider . . . . met at ———, at —— o'clock.

——— ——— was chosen Chairman, and ——— ——— Secretary.

After prayer by ——— ———, the Chairman stated the object of the Convention to be . . . .

[Then follows a record of proceedings.]

Adjourned or dissolved.

——— ——— *Chairman.*
——— ——— *Secretary.*

NOTE.—The rules of order for all meetings of business, whether churches, councils, conventions, or committees, are substantially the same. But each body has a right to form rules for itself, and decide its own order of business.

---

11. *Form of License.*

It is customary for churches to give a *license* to those who are believed to have been called to preach the Gospel, but are not yet ready to be ordained and enter fully upon the work of the ministry.

The following is a form which may be varied according to circumstances.

License.[1]

This certifies that Brother ——— ——— is a member of the ——— ——— church, in good standing, and held by us in high esteem; and believing him to have been called of God to the

[1] See First Part, chap. vii. 8.

work of the Gospel ministry, we hereby give him our entire and cordial approbation in the improvement of his gifts, by preaching the Gospel as Providence may afford him an opportunity, praying the great Head of the church to endow him with all needful grace, and crown his labors with abundant success.

Done by order of the church, This day, May ——, 18—.

—— —— *Pastor.*

—— —— *Clerk.*

---

12. *Certificate of Ordination.*

This certifies, that our Brother —— —— was publicly ordained and set apart to the work of the Gospel ministry, with prayer, and the laying on of hands, by the ministers, according to the usages of Baptist churches, on May —, 18—.

That he was called to ordination by the —— Church, of which he was a member, and which, after full and sufficient opportunity to judge of his gifts, were agreed in the opinion, that he was called of God to the work of the ministry.

That —— churches were represented in the council, by —— ministers, and —— laymen, and that after a full, fair, and deliberate examination, being satisfied on all points, the council did unanimously recommend his ordination.

That our Brother ——— ——— did accordingly receive the full, entire, and hearty approbation of the council, in his officially entering upon the work of the ministry, administering the ordinances of the Gospel, and performing all those duties, and enjoying all those privileges to which a minister of Christ is called.

And may the blessing of the great Head of the Church attend him, crown his labors with abundant success, and make him an honored instrument of good to Zion and the world.

——— ——— *Moderator.*
——— ——— *Clerk.*

NEW YORK, *Sept.* —, 18—.

CHAPTER IX.

BENEVOLENT SOCIETIES.

EVERY member of a church should not only be familiar with the state of his own church, but should also have a general knowledge of what is being done in his denomination for the welfare of humanity and the conversion of the world. He ought to understand the objects and operations of the various benevolent societies for the spread of the Gospel, and to the extent of his ability aid them in their good work. The following are the principal benevolent societies of the Baptist denomination:

1. *Missionary Union.* 1814.

In the month of February, 1812, Rev. Adoniram Judson and Rev. Luther Rice, sailed from Salem, Mass., as missionaries for Asia, under the patronage of the Board of Commissioners for Foreign Missions, which had been organized in 1810. Mr. Judson and Mr. Rice, with their wives, having experienced a change in their opinions respecting the ordinance of baptism, on reaching India connected themselves with the Baptists, and resigning their connection with the board of commissioners, sent back an appeal to the Baptists of America for support.

Meeting with much difficulty in their endea vors to establish a mission, Mr. Rice returned to America, to excite if possible a deeper interest on behalf of the heathen, while Mr. Judson, in a very providential manner, and contrary to all his previous plans, entered Burmah, and arrived at Rangoon, July, 1813.

These events deeply aroused the attention of American Baptists, and produced a general conviction that immediate efforts should be made to organize a society for the support of foreign missions. Accordingly a convention was called, composed of delegates from churches and associations. This convention met in Philadelphia May 18, 1814, when the "Triennial Convention" was formed, under the name of "The General Missionary Convention of the Baptist Denomination in the United States of America for Foreign Missions." This society continued to operate efficiently until November, 1845, when at a special meeting held in New York, various changes were made in its constitution and the mode of its operations, and the name changed to that of "American Baptist Missionary Union," which it still retains.

At the last annual meeting, held in Philadelphia, May, 1858, the society reported for the year then just closed, $97,808 collected, and $97,797 expended; 81 missionaries and 246 native assistants; 107 missions, and 779 out stations; 312 churches; 22,669 church members, about 14,000 of whom are in Asia and 7,000 in Europe. About 3,000 baptisms were reported during the past year. These missions are in Burmah, Assam, Siam, Arracan, China, France, and Germany, and in three tribes of American Indians. Those in Asia are chiefly in Burmah, and those in Europe mostly in Germany.

The Union meets annually, as does its Board, but the administration of its affairs is chiefly in the hands of the Executive Committee, which holds weekly meetings, and is located in Boston.

2. *American Baptist Publication Society.* 1824.

The American Baptist Publication Society grew out of the "Baptist General Tract Society," which was formed at Washington, D. C., Feb. 20, 1824. The Tract Society itself grew out of a concurrence of providential circumstances, evidently designed to foster a gracious enterprise for the good of society. Rev. Noah Davis,

Rev. J. D. Knowles, and Rev. Dr. Staughton, were chiefly instrumental in its origination.

During its first year, this Society published nineteen tracts, containing, in all, fifty-six pages, of which 86,000 copies, in the aggregate, were circulated. In 1826, the society was transferred to Philadelphia, as better calculated for the centre of its operations. In 1827, the publication of a monthly magazine was commenced, with the title of Baptist Tract Magazine. At length a necessity for *books* became apparent, to supply Sabbath-school libraries, and furnish religious reading for families. Books of a denominational character, such as other societies would not, and private publishers could not, at the time, well supply, were called for.

At the sixteenth anniversary, held with the Tabernacle church in New York, April, 1840, the Society was reorganized on a broader basis, and called the "American Baptist Publication Society," for the publication of a denominational and general religious literature. During the previous sixteen years of its existence, 160 different tracts had been published, of which about 54,000,000 pages had been circulated at an expense of not far from $86,000. A fund for the erection of a Tract House had been raised amounting to nearly $10,000.

After its reorganization the Society extended its operations, and pursued them with increased vigor. Particularly did the work of *Colportage* receive great attention. In 1855 the constitution was still further amended, and in 1856 the "New England Sunday School Union," a society similar in character and aim, was merged in this. It deserved to be noticed that as early as 1811, a society called the "Evangelical Tract Society," was organized by the Baptists in Boston, and from that time onward Boston had been the centre of operations in the department of religious publication by the Baptists, but which was chiefly confined to New England.

From the last report of the Publication Society, it appears that during the year previous to May 1858, $60,585 were collected, and $60,430 were disbursed. During the year, fifty-three colporters had been employed, whose aggregate labors amounted to more than twenty-seven years: 20,052 volumes sold, 4,996 volumes given away; 187,184 pages of tracts distributed; 3,263 sermons preached, 1,107 prayer-meetings held, 802 converts baptized, eighteen churches formed, twenty-nine Sabbath-schools organized. Of the "Young Reaper," a periodical for Sunday schools, 70,000 copies were issued monthly.

3. *Home Mission Society.* 1832.

Strictly speaking, the first society organized by American Baptists for missionary purposes, was a *home mission* society. This was the "Massachusetts Baptist Missionary Society," organized in 1802, "to furnish occasional preaching, and to promote the knowledge of evangelical truth in the new settlements within the United States, or further, if circumstances should render it proper." Other societies were subsequently formed, as the "New York Baptist Missionary Society." These continued for many years to perform efficient service in the cause of home evangelization. But they were, to a great degree, local in their operations, and restricted in their membership; they did not command the sympathies and the coöperation of the denomination generally. A national society was needed.

Chiefly through the efforts of Baptists in Boston, an exploration of the new States and territoriee was undertaken, with a view to organize a society for more comprehensive operations. This work of exploration was performed by Rev. Jonathan Going, and was so efficiently done, and the necessity of more extended missionary efforts so earnestly pressed upon the churches as to lead to the organization of the present society.

Preliminary steps having been taken, the "American Baptist Home Mission Society," was organized by a convention called for that purpose, April 27, 1832.

The Board is located in New York, and holds monthly meetings, the Society itself meeting annually. At its last anniversary, in May, 1858, the Society reported $43,126 received during the year then just closed; $47,634 disbursed in the same time. During that year, 93 missionaries and 6 collecting agents had been employed. These missionaries were distributed in 16 states, territories and provinces. Of these, also, twenty preached the Gospel in eight different languages besides the English. The number of stations and out-stations 247, and an aggregate of labor equal to that of one man for 64 years. Conversions during the year about 1,000; of whom 593 were baptized into the fellowship of churches; and 27 new churches were organized.

4. *American and Foreign Bible Society.* 1838.

Previous to the year 1837, American Baptists had coöperated with the American Bible Society in their work of translating and distributing the word of God among the heathen. The American Bible Society being a union society, composed of and sustained by all evangelical Christians, it was thought better to pass contributions for Bible circulation through that society, than to organize another.

Rev. Mr. Pearce and Rev. Mr. Yates, Baptist missionaries in India, had completed a translation of the Scriptures into Bengalee, acknowledged to be one of the best ever made into a foreign tongue. This translation the British and Foreign Bible Society refused to assist them in the printing and circulation of, not because it was not *faithful*, but because it rendered the word *baptize* by a word meaning to *dip*. In 1835, a letter was received by the American Bible Society from Mr. Pearce, inquiring if that society would aid them where the British society had refused. These missionaries in Calcutta knew that American Baptists contributed large sums of money to the treasury of the American Bible Society, and doubtless supposed they would be willing to appropriate a part of it to aid the Baptist missions in India. In this, however, they were mistaken.

During about one year the Board of the American Society debated the propriety of granting the request. At length they decided to refuse the aid asked for, and at the following anniversary the Society sanctioned the action of the Board, though the Baptist members both of the

Board and of the Society, earnestly protested against such action, as most unjust, unreasonable, and inexpedient.

It appears that Baptists had contributed to the funds of this society nearly $45,000 in legacies alone, and probably nearly as much more in other ways. And yet, in return, all the Society had ever appropriated for the aid of Baptists was $28,450, more than $1,200 of which was given in Bibles, and not in money.

Such being the case, the pastors and members of the churches resolved that they would have a Bible Society of their own, and no longer support one which refused assistance to their own brethren for no other reason than because their translation was too faithful to the original.

May 12, 1836, a large convention met in the Oliver street church, New York, and after discussion, proceeded to organize the American and Foreign Bible Society. Rev. Spencer H. Cone, who had been prominent in these proceedings, was its first president, and for many years continued to fill that office; and William Colgate, Esq., was for a similar period its treasurer. The first annual meeting of the Society was held in Philadelphia, May 1, 1837. The report of the treasurer shows that during the first year of its existence over $21,000 were contributed for its use. The Society continued its operations with increasing interest and success. It applied to the legislature of New York for a charter, but was met by most decided and persevering opposion from the American Bible Society, and from other sources, until in 1848 a charter was secured and accepted.

The Society meets annually; the Board is located in New York, and holds monthly meetings. Its funds are appropiated to print and circulate the sacred Scriptures, and to sustain Bible reading colporters. Its fields are in America, Canada, New Mexico, Germany, Greece, China, and Burmah. During the year previous to May, 1858, the Society has received $40,189 for its general purposes, and expended $45,293. About $12,000 towards the expense of the new Bible House, have also been collected. Thirteen colporters are sustained in Germany. There were 485 baptisms reported during the year.

5. *American Baptist Free Mission Society.* 1843.

The organization of the Free Mission Society was owing to a desire on the part of those who engaged in it, to have a society for the purpose of missions, so entirely free from every suspicion of connection or sympathy with slavery, as not to receive money to its treasury contributed by slaveholders, or which was the known avails of slavery. Such persons were not altogether satisfied with existing societies in this respect, and desired one which should be distinctly and plainly understood on that point.

A preliminary meeting was held in the Tremont Chapel, Boston, May 4, 1843, when a committee was appointed to draft a constitution, and then adjourn till May 31, 1843. At that time the convention assembled in the same place, and an organization was effected under the name of the "American and Foreign Baptist Missionary Society," which name was subsequently changed to that which it now bears. In June, 1846, the Society was chartered by the legislature of Maine, which charter was accepted and adopted at a special meeting held in Utica in November following.

The operations of the Society have been limited. It has, however, had missionaries in Hayti, Canada, and several western States, and is now sustaining several in Burmah. It issues a weekly religious paper, published in the city of New York, called the "American Baptist." The receipts of the Society in its various operations, for the year closing May, 1857, were a little more than $13,000, and its expenditure $7,329, leaving some $5,700 in the treasury

The Board is now located in the city of New York.

6. *The Southern Baptist Convention.* 1845.

For many years, Baptists throughout the United States, without sectional distinctions, had coöperated in the work of missions. But more recently, the question of slavery had been a source of dissatisfaction and discontent between the brethren and churches North and South. At length, the Board of the Triennial Convention at Boston (now the Missionary Union), in reply to some interrogatories from Alabama, said in substance, that they could not appoint as a missionary, one who owned slaves, and insisted on holding them as property. This state of feeling, and these frequent mutual irritations, led the churches at the South to conclude that they could best perform the missionary work devolving on them by operating separately from the northern churches.

Accordingly, in response to a call from the Board of the Virginia Foreign Baptist Missionary Society, a Convention met in Augusta, Georgia, May 8, 1845. This Convention was composed of delegates from churches, missionary societies, and other religious bodies of Baptists, chiefly at the South. After a presentation of the whole subject by a committee, the "Southern Baptist Convention" was organized. Rev. William B. Johnson, D.D., was its first president, and continued for several years to fill that office. The Convention at first was *triennial*, but afterwards became *biennial* as it continues still to be.

The Convention meets every two years at such places as may be agreed upon. It has a Foreign Missionary Board located in Richmond, Virginia; a Domestic Missionary Board located in Marion, Alabama; a Bible Board located in Nashville, Tennessee. These Boards hold annual meetings at such places as they may select.

By the sixth biennial report of the Convention, made at its meeting in Louisville, Kentucky, May 8, 1857, there was reported by the Domestic Board, $40,420 collected from all sources during the preceding year, and about $37,300 expended. By the Foreign Missionary Board, in the same time, about $32,000 collected, and about 33,000 expended. This is expended chiefly on different missions in Africa, but a part of it in China. The Bible Board report about $33,000 collected, and about 31,000 expended, chiefly in home distribution. Making an aggregate of about $100,000 yearly expended in missionary operations in Africa, China, and the southern and western States.

7. *Southern Baptist Publication Society.* 1847.

The Southern Baptist Publication Society was organized at Savannah, Georgia, May 13, 1847, and arose out of the disturbed state of feeling on the question of slavery, existing between the North and South, as connected with missionary and general benevolent efforts. The South, believing they could no longer coöperate with the North in existing societies, had already created organizations for missionary work, at home and abroad.

Attention was next called to their existing sources of religious literature. The Publication Society, located at Philadelphia, had given the South no cause for complaints by the course it had pursued, still the prevailing sentiment demanded a Southern Society. The first annual report of its board says, "The common sentiment was, give us a Southern Society, or we will patronize none; the common demand was for a literature adapted to the genius of our own institutions, thriving upon our own soil, fostered and cherished by our own intellect."

Accordingly, and pursuant to a call issued the

previous year, by the Central Association of Georgia, delegates met in Savannah, May 13, 1847, organized this society, and entered upon the work of preparing and publishing religious books and tracts. The first annual report shows about $2,700 received into the treasury the first year, and a little more than that sum disbursed. By the report of the year closing with May, 1858, the receipts from all sources were $9,794 for that year, and the expenditures $9,159. During the ten years of its operations, the society had issued 222,175 volumes of its different works, being an aggregate of more than 82,000,000 pages, while several new works were in preparation, and the operations of the Society rapidly extending.

The Society holds annual meetings, and its affairs are administered by a board located in Charleston, S. C.

8. *Other Societies.*

Education Societies.—In various states and sections of the country are education Societies, chiefly for the purpose of aiding indigent, but worthy young men, to procure an Education preparatory to entering upon the work of the Gospel ministry. The funds of these societies are supplied by contributions from churches and individuals for this purpose. The amounts thus furnished to beneficiaries are, usually, only sufficient to meet the expense of their board and tuition. Other necessary expenses are met by the student's own efforts, and the exercise of a rigid economy.

These benefactions are bestowed only on those of undoubted worth and merit, and only after they have been recommended by the churches of which they are members. It is to be expected that in some instances, young men thus aided may disappoint the hopes of their friends and patrons; but many of the most distinguished and useful of our ministers, have risen from obscurity to positions of honor and influence, by the timely and judicious assistance of these societies.

Historical Societies.—There are in the United States several Baptist Historical Societies, the object of which is the collection and preservation of such facts as shall form material, at some future time, for a clear and comprehensive history of the denomination. The early history of the churches and ministers, their trials and successes, the struggles and triumphs of their sentiments, especially their relation to religious freedom, all these merit a permanent record.

The labors, sufferings, and achievements of the

fathers should be carefully gathered and guarded, and transmitted to the children, to stimulate their zeal, and inspire their gratitude. Many facts which now would be regarded as scarcely worthy of note, would, if preserved, be cherished by future generations as a precious legacy.

American Bible Union.—The American Bi ble Union, though not a Baptist Society, yet, as it was originated by Baptists, and as that denomi nation is more largely represented in its board of officers and its membership than any other, it may with propriety be mentioned here.

The *object* of the Bible Union as presented by its constitution, is to procure accurate and faithful translations of the Holy Scriptures, in all languages. Its labors thus far, however, have been mainly directed to secure a corrected version of the English Scriptures. It is conceded that in the common version of the Bible, there exists various errors and mistakes, some of which arose from the condition of biblical literature at the time the translation was made, some from the restrictions under which the translators were placed, and some from changes in the English language since that time. Some of these errors are important, many of them are unimportant; nevertheless, the Word of God should be trans lated from the inspired originals, into all languages, with the greatest fidelity, and the nearest approach to perfection which it is possible for human learning and piety to attain. It will be observed that the Union embraces, also, in its constitutional provisions, the design of circulating, as well as of translating, the Bible in all languages.

The *history* of the Bible Union goes back to June 10, 1850, at which time its organization took place. The Am. & For. Bible Society had been called into existence for the purpose of procuring faithful versions of the Scriptures in foreign tongues, but confined its issues and circulation of the English Scriptures to the common version. Some of the prominent members of that society believed that they ought to attempt to secure an accurate translation of the Bible in their own as well as in other languages. Foremost among those was the venerable Dr. Cone, who, more than any other man, had been prominent in the formation of the Society, and in all of its operations. The large majority of the members, however, while they saw and conceded the importance of the work itself, did not think that Society should undertake the translation or revision of the English Scriptures.

At the anniversary of the Am. & For. Bible

Society, held in the city of New York, in May, 1850, this question came up, and after a protracted discussion, the Society voted to confine its labors in the circulation of the English Scriptures to the common version, as it had previously done. This was regarded, by the members who took a different view of the question, as binding the Society to a policy which they could not approve. Dr. Cone was reëlected president, but declined to accept. On the 27th of the same month, a preliminary meeting was held, and on June 10, 1850, at a meeting held in the Mulbury St. Tabernacle, in New York, the Bible Union was organized. Dr. Cone was elected president, and so continued till his death. Wm. H. Wykoff was chosen corresponding secretary, and William Colgate treasurer.

The members and officers of the Union are connected with different denominations. Its Board is located in New York. Its anniversary is held in the month of October. It has had employed at various times a considerable number of translators, or revisors, engaged upon the English Scriptures. These are mostly in this country, and are connected with different denominations. The treasurer's report for the first four months of the society's existence, showed $5,595 received. The second annual report was

$14,495; the third, $16,799. The report for 1858, shows that $35,376 were raised and expended during the year. Of this sum, $17,561 were expended on the department of English Scriptures, something more than $10,000 as salaries and expenses of agents, officers and assistants, and the balance in various items.

THE END.

www.ingramcontent.com/pod-product-compliance
Lightning Source LLC
LaVergne TN
LVHW010221110826
845151LV00004B/1163
9781425525415